1

Psychological Triggers:

The Hidden Influences Behind Our Actions, Thoughts, and Behaviors. Human Nature and Why We Do What We Do.

By Peter Hollins,
Author and Researcher at
peterhollins.com

Table of Contents

Chapter 1. Introduction to Psychological Triggers

More often than we'd like to admit, we act against our own interests. Just looking at your current day or week, how many times have you chosen to engage in some activity at your own expense, knowing it's not what you should be doing? You may even be doing it right now by reading this!

Maybe that's not you. You might be thinking, "Nope, not me. I'm as logical and rational as they come!" That might be true, but you are still human and subject to human impulses.

Consider the following. You've been texting or chatting with someone that you're romantically interested in. Things appear to be going well. In fact, you've made jokes about visiting Europe together in the summer. However, suddenly, they disappear from sight and, for all intents and purposes, go radio silent on you. Do you rationally and logically conclude that they have lost interest and immediately move on, or do you flail about, wondering if they got hit by a hurricane that prevented them from replying to you?

Does something about your love interest being relatively unavailable trigger some instinct in you that makes you reach out and desire more? Might you be tempted to carry out impulsive, objectively unstable actions to settle your uncertainty?

Let's take it one step further. You see a homeless adult begging on the sidewalk. You might be able to look past this, depending on how accustomed you are to such sights. You might even be able to ignore it completely. Now replace that adult with two children, both blind. They are crying for their mother, who they claim was taken from them, leaving them to fend for themselves. To boot, they have a tiny kitten with them, who is meowing loudly out of hunger. It's quite a heart-wrenching scene.

Do your feelings change based on the emotions that such a scene evokes? Do you feel some sort of natural impulse to ease this group's suffering based on sympathy or pity?

In both of these circumstances, you probably made up your mind at first and then flipped the opposite way once your emotions were put into play. These are the small ways in which we are pushed and pulled in our daily lives. For lack of a better term, we can refer to them as *psychological triggers*—things that tug on our heartstrings and other instincts and demand action. They create impulses in us to act immediately and often in irrational ways. They are the all-too-human tendencies of leaping before looking, and they've been bred into us for thousands of years. More often than not, and certainly more than often than we would like to admit, they dictate our actions.

You may not think much of them, but once you begin to realize just how widespread and common psychological triggers really are in your life, you may even begin to question whether or not you have free will. The above examples were about emotions and emotional arousal. When our minds are clouded with rage or fear, it's clear that we seek fast action, not accurate or even smart behavior.

You'll see this pattern repeated in just about every area of your life. That's because psychological triggers can be just about anything, from the people around you, to the environment you inhabit, our natural human instincts and biological drives, and, yes, every single emotion.

Philosophers have often wondered about the nature of our decisions. Some posit that our fates are preordained and that we don't really have free will. Scientists prefer to propose that we are products of our environments or past experiences. Psychologists have observed that people sometimes act first, then create justifications for their actions after the fact. So why do we do what we do—*really*?

That question is what I sought to research and discuss in this book. Our conception of free will—the fact that we can make decisions in a vacuum despite our circumstances—does it exist? Or are we inevitably affected and triggered by external and subconscious circumstances, even those that aren't present and haven't been for many years? The former possibility is certainly more attractive, but unfortunately, most signs point to the latter. Therapists are thrilled at this because that's their bread and butter, but what does it mean for the rest of us?

Humans can be said to be an inventory of experiences from which we make judgments. With the help of this book, you'll be able to pick out and identify some of what happens in between experiences and judgments—the perceptions, triggers, and emotions that make us who we are. Psychological triggers may dictate your life, but at least we can learn to insulate ourselves against some of the more irrational and self-defeating impulses we all experience.

Filled with good intentions, we make plans for our lives that don't always work. Despite wanting one thing, we choose another. We commit, make promises, set goals. And yet we're often unhappy, unfulfilled, confused. How do we go astray in our lives? What leads us to make questionable or bad choices? What causes us to pursue erroneous lines of thought that result in faulty conclusions?

Most of the time in our lives, we generally know what we should be doing. We even know what we shouldn't be doing. So why aren't we partaking in what we know is good for us and avoiding what we know is bad? Are we just piles of impulses instead of a functional brain?

Why do we act against our own interests so frequently? These questions are perhaps some of the most commonly asked in psychology, philosophy, and everyday life, and have occupied mankind more or less since the beginning. The answer is simple: psychological triggers. And this is what this book serves to investigate.

We live under the pretense that all humans, as we're told, have free will. We never really question this premise. The principle of free will declares we make our own choices under our own discretion, independently of the influence of outside factors or the requirements of the rest of the world.

In reality, we have much less control over our own decisions and actions than we believe. We don't have true free will. Often ,we're not even aware of all the ways we are unaware. Instead, we are composites of psychological triggers that dictate our decisions and regulate our emotions. Of course, we are capable of making rational decisions, but for most of our recorded (and unrecorded) history, that hasn't been what's kept us alive and thriving.

It's impossible to define or even count how we're affected by factors we don't control or have awareness of. So many of these triggers accumulate in the subconscious throughout the course of our lives without any sense of rhyme or reason. These forces are so powerful that they make logic and rationality the exceptions, not the rule.

Even though psychological triggers come from the brain, they actually serve to bypass active thought. They force us to make decisions from a reactionary, emotional standpoint, away from the logic and reasoning the brain supposedly supports. Psychological triggers produce thoughts and behaviors that often result in dreadful decisions and results.

It's as though we were two people—one logical, rational being with free will operating in plain sight of conscious awareness, and one who's really pulling all the strings beneath, hidden in the unconscious and unacknowledged mechanisms that actually inform our everyday behavior.

How can psychological triggers stoke the ego, seduce people away from rational thinking, and produce disastrous consequences? There's a fairly recent episode that was particularly illuminative about the driving forces behind people's behavior. This is what can happen when we are driven by our impulses and triggers instead of rational thought.

In 2017 a young entrepreneur had a vision for a two-day music festival. He put together a social media campaign, promising superstar performers, gourmet food, and luxurious accommodations for everyone who bought a pass. The festival ran into a lot of snags in the planning stage. At one point some advisors floated the idea of postponing the festival for a year so they could get their ducks in a row and execute a great show. And for a while, the organizers agreed to make that the plan of action.

But at the very last minute—for reasons that are unexplained but obviously were very impulsive—they changed their minds and went ahead with plans to put the show on at its original time. "Let's just do it and be legends, man," one of the organizers was reported to say.

What impulse triggered this sudden change? An appeal to the ego? Impatience? Greed? Pride? The psychological concept of sunk costs? It could have been any or all of those. But when the decision to go ahead was made, preparations were at such a low point that the weekend was almost canceled. Instead, for whatever reason, it wasn't, which meant the organizers had to hurry up and make some quick decisions on their feet. They thought they could pull it off.

They didn't.

On the weekend of the show, attendees flew to the island in the Bahamas. At first, they were directed to an "impromptu beach party." At the venue, one band of local musicians finally took the stage, hardly a superstar act. They played for a few hours. They were the only musicians to play the festival.

A little while later the organizers announced that the festival was being postponed, and they promised to fly all the attendees back to the States as soon as they could. There were several reports of mishandled luggage, no housing for guests, no portable toilets, no water, no useable mattresses, and no Internet service. There *was* food, though: processed American cheese on wheat bread and a couple of lettuce leaves. Reporters compared the scene to something out of *The Hunger Games.*

The fallout? Multiple lawsuits against the festival organizers, an investigation by the FBI, and the entrepreneur pleading guilty to wire fraud.

Not knowing any of the principals, we can't offer much of an opinion on what kind of emotional person the creator was and what drove him. But think of that impulsive statement: "Let's just do it and be legends." That could be indicative of several emotional stances: hubris, excessive ambition, unchecked optimism, and maybe even contempt or malice.

Whatever the cause, it set off a chain of events that turned out to be a disaster on every conceivable front. It flattened careers and fatally embarrassed several high-profile celebrities and partners, all because one guy said, "Screw it. Let's be legends." And, well, in a way I suppose they are.

This demonstrates how psychological triggers can lay plans to waste. At various junctures in this story, there were opportunities to break the flow of thought and think logically. If all parties involved kept their rational states of mind intact throughout the whole process, they would have approached the logistical problems realistically and adjusted their strategy. Truth be told, the festival should have been canceled right at the point where advisers were suggesting it.

But instead of the advice winning out, something in the organizers' headspace—pride, ego, fear?—triggered the irrational response to "be legends." The impetus barreled through all logic and analysis and caused them to make a fatally bad choice.

We hold up rationality, reason, sense, and logic as ideal elements that encompass the way things "should be done." But are they actually *contrary* to our nature? Evolutionary scientists, researchers, and psychologists indicate that they very well may be, and their reasons are compelling.

If we are in fact driven in the main by unconscious, irrational or hidden forces, it makes sense that it's *here* that we should focus our attention when considering how to be more effective people with more developed self-determination and discipline.

Risk Detection

In a way, psychological triggers are simply part of evolution. The core of evolutional thought is the concept of "survival of the fittest": the types of beings that were best able to adapt and endure changes in their environments were the ones who survived. A major element of a species' survival is its ability to assess potential threats or hazards—what we call *risk detection*.

Nowadays we can analyze risk far in advance, but we haven't always had that luxury. Risks presented themselves more suddenly in eras before our own. Dealing with them required instant, on-the-spot judgment and decision made with little or no information. Many of these quick decisions were matters of life and death, and there was no back data to consult or historical models to emulate. Over time, these reflexes became instinctual to us and were beneficial more often than not.

The best thing about these impulses is also the worst thing about them: they are knee-jerk, instant and require no higher cognitive power. We have, for better and worse, retained that reflex to the present day. Our biological makeup is trained for thinking and acting on our feet, relying on our instincts for survival. That's not a bad thing in and of itself, and sometimes it even works. But it's designed to be fast rather than accurate.

Certainly, it's worked for our benefit in terms of evolution. We're more *able* to react quickly to modern complications because of how we've been conditioned in earlier, different environments. But more often than not, we don't have every bit of information we need to make a truly logical, 100 percent sound decision. Evolution has favored quick, good-enough responses over slower, better-quality ones.

It's not to say that this is always a bad trade to make; spending too long on deliberation also has its costs and risks. There's the other extreme of wasting excessive time considering the nuts and bolts of a decision to the point that we overthink so much that we don't act. We commonly call this "analysis paralysis." For instance, an office worker could spend so much time deciding on a document format that they miss a deadline.

Thankfully, now we don't always have to go into jungle survival mode. Humans of the present have more time to analyze whether our initial "gut" feelings are right or wrong, especially when we have hard data and past results to advise us. But it's not possible to do that with every situation we encounter. The "gut" doesn't compute the math or run scenarios for sudden events—and it's subject to our cognitive biases, those errors in judgment we make from our personal preferences or beliefs. Despite having greater access to information and more time to consider it, we still tend to make stupid decisions.

Humans in their modern form have only been around for about 200,000 years. Before that, our ancestors lived in various forms with less developed brains yet more developed survival instincts. Civilization, in which we've finally tried to establish some kind of order and write down some rules, has only been here for 6,000 to 10,000 years—depending on who you ask.

The math says, and evolutionists will confirm, that for the huge majority of human existence we've lived off our instincts. It's noteworthy that this technique has worked for as long as it has, and has largely made us who we are today. The families of our distant ancestors were fairly small because of the inherent risks of growing larger.

We may not be as savage anymore (not all of us, anyway), but our brains still have that intuitive drive, even if we're swilling lattés instead of spearing woolly mammoths. Parents' intuition kicks in when they're walking with their children and they see a person they perceive as sketchy approaching them; they hustle their kids off to one side just in case. Or if we're feeling extra hungry in the drive-thru lane at a fast-food joint, we could get impatient if the cars in front of us are taking too long. We might even honk.

Whether through quick learning or careful planning, risk detection has implanted more than cautionary approaches in our psyches—it's also helped form psychological triggers that can go off even without external prompting. Instincts that formerly helped us immensely now seize control at inopportune moments and influence us in negative ways. Free will isn't always as available as we think.

Phobias

Humans also cede control to phobias, which, strictly defined, are irrational fears of (or aversion to) certain things or conditions. Phobias are the ultimate psychological triggers. They're often, though not always, based on illogical or groundless anxieties and, as such, result in the destruction of our rational and analytical thought processes. These are the extreme versions of risk detection dictating our actions and behaviors.

We're familiar with the most common phobias: acrophobia is fear of heights, claustrophobia is fear of tight spaces, aviophobia is fear of flight. But even though many phobias are irrational, they don't all spring from manufactured threats or false alarms. Again, they have roots in our evolutionary development.

For example, take two of our favorite phobias: arachnophobia and ophidiophobia—the fears of spiders and snakes, respectively. Our ancestors contended with their own fears of these creatures and had to develop solutions to avoid them to keep themselves alive. In fact, those old distant phobias from ages ago still keep us from completely adapting to contemporary life. Certain conditions still bring out irrational fears that haven't yet developed beyond our caveman years.

Phobias take us outside of rational thought and rob us of free will. Many of us recoil in terror when we see a spider in the attic or even a harmless garter snake in the grass. The sight of both of those creatures produces acute dread, even if they're perfectly safe to be around. Nobody has such a frightened reaction, though, when they see a parked car. Most of us see cars every day and don't feel a single shred of panic. In fact, there isn't even a *name* for the phobia of cars in general (only the fear of *riding in* a car has a name, which for the record is amaxophobia).

But in 2016, almost 37,500 people were killed in US car accidents. Meanwhile, an average of 11.6 Americans die from spider and snake bites each year—combined. The math is hilarious: using those figures for calculation, 3,232 times more people die in car wrecks than bites from creepy things. Between cars, spiders, and snakes, there's no contest as to which ones are the real killing machines: the ones with four wheels.

So why are we so deathly afraid at the sight of spiders and snakes but not cars? The only answer that makes any sense is the evolutionary one. Spiders and snakes *were* legitimate menaces to society at one time, maybe even for most of the era of human existence. They have become ingrained in our psyches as enormous risks to avoid at all costs. Car wreck fatalities have only been around since the invention of motorized vehicles—roughly the 1890s, which is practically yesterday in terms of human consciousness. In the meantime, medical advances have reduced the chance of getting killed by a spider or snake to almost zero.

But spiders and snakes still get the bad rap from our brains, which haven't gotten over our prehistoric phobias. Our fear of those critters is so enmeshed in our biological chemistry that it may be many more millennia before evolution processes it out, if it ever does.

Importantly, it doesn't really matter what your free will or determination tells you to do—you may know on an intellectual level that a snake or spider is not actually venomous or dangerous in any way, and *still* feel panic on seeing it. Such is the power of evolutionarily programmed phobias and instincts.

American psychologist Martin Seligman composed a paper called "Phobias and Preparedness" in 1971, and it's had a major impact on the psychological community ever since. Seligman noted that we almost never fear modern-world things like guns, electricity outlets, or hammers, even though such items can and do cause immediate and fatal injury. But our fears of fire, water, insects, and heights endure, even if they're innocuous or easy to avoid.

This is because, Seligman argues, those things *did* pose a clear and present danger to ancient humans. Even as our species evolved and we found ways to control those old threats—with firehoses, boats, bug spray, and safety restraints—many people still fear them. And once again, this eliminates our ability to think rationally: we don't fear what is *truly* dangerous. This is remarkable because it's another way we have been programmed to think irrationally—and yet this irrationality doesn't extend far enough in some cases! It fails us by making us overreact at harmless situations, but completely underestimate truly dangerous ones.

Seligman hinted that our phobias are inflated modifications of real dangers that existed eons ago. Evolution hasn't yet processed those fears out of our bloodline. They're still hard-wired into our systems, and we humans are almost organically inclined to develop those phobias. They're a set of psychological triggers you get for absolutely free upon your arrival on Earth. Thanks, Darwin!

Seligman's work also hints at an idea we'll be returning to again and again in this book: just because instincts, gut feelings, knee-jerk reactions, biases and unconscious urges are there for some reason or other (i.e. they're "natural"), this doesn't mean they're always good for us, and can't be questioned, challenged or upgraded.

Anxiety and Fear

As we've seen, our ancestors used fear as a sort of internal defense mechanism—it protected them and helped them survive. They were grateful that their brains blacked out when risks were present and made them act quickly. It still helps.

Indeed, one study found that 77 percent of mothers whose children feared water said their children were scared the first time they ever saw larger bodies of water, like pools or lakes. This was especially true the farther away the families lived from the ocean. Another study, one which took many years to complete, found that kids who were scared of heights were much less likely to suffer from falls when they were older. These children were guarded by their fears—their anxieties were natural, practically inborn qualities that kept them from danger into adulthood.

Ancient humans may have paid the price with occasional irrational decisions, but fear tended to be their best friend in most cases. Fear is one of the most powerful psychological triggers in the same way that punishments create motivation, and Machiavelli's book on ruthless governance, *The Prince*, became so infamous.

Fear is truly one of the strongest psychological triggers because it completely overrides our brains and sends us into action. Fear is what causes us to drop absolutely everything in the interest of self-preservation in one way or another. It sharpens our senses and tells us to sit up and pay attention, or act to protect ourselves.

Unfortunately for us, most causes of modern fears are rather misleading and unimportant. We could listen completely to our fears and never question them, letting them guide our every decision and the course of our lives... or we could become curious about the mechanism of fear itself and intelligently decide whether it's working in our best interests.

For many, for example, feelings of hunger will cause us to grow irrational and angry.

This stems from the fear our primitive ancestors had about starving to death. This negative association with hunger used to keep us alive in whatever way possible. Before they learned to hunt, our ancestors were scavengers. Instead of going to the dirty business of killing prey, they'd let an apex do it. The scavengers patiently watched the tiger dine on its kill until the beast finally got full and walked away.

At that point, the scavengers ran over to the carcass and consumed as much of the leftovers as they possibly could before another wild creature came around and they had to run off. It wasn't ice cream, frosted cupcakes, or cheese puffs, but it was still binge-eating. And now, we simply binge-eat to the brink of obesity due to subconscious associations with hunger.

Our psyche tells us we have to get as much as we can until the next apex predator (or, more likely, roommate or spouse) comes around. It's also why our eating binges tend to feature high-calorie, high-carb, or high-sugar foods—health ramifications aside, that stuff satisfies us and fills us up. It also explains the inclination some people have to hoard food: our ancestors had to store quite a bit away for seasons when predators didn't hunt so much.

It doesn't matter if you're seriously overweight and your feelings of "hunger" are not true physiological hunger at all. The inherited impulse to behave as your ancestors did can override any rational decision, i.e. "I only ate an hour ago, I'm not really hungry, I'm just bored. I can wait till dinner, and I'm not going to die if I do..."

The big takeaway from this discussion is that anxieties and fears create a frame of mind in which we feel we have to act immediately to gain pleasure and avoid punishment. We enter into a heightened state of emergency in which we believe we must take action now. It's not about the *correct* action, the moral action, or the pleasurable action. It's about the most immediate action. It's in that vulnerable state that psychological triggers are most powerful—and most dangerous.

In the beginning of the chapter we asked, why do people act against their best interests? Why do we make plans and then go against them later? The answer is here: in the heat of the moment, your psychological triggers overwhelmed your higher critical thinking skills. You can put the blame squarely on your limbic system and amygdala, as they deal with fear and anxiety. They're the controllers of our automatic and subconscious responses, and they're a little too engaged for our own good.

The limbic system administers the aspects of our emotional responses connected with memory and stimulation. A few parts of the limbic system have important roles in the development of psychological triggers, like the hypothalamus and the hippocampus. But it's the amygdala that really goes overboard with the drama.

Every time the amygdala gets info about an imminent threat, it goes into overdrive. And—this is very important—it does so whether it's an *actual* threat or a *perceived* threat. Your amygdala snaps into action whether there's a real truck headed straight toward you or if it merely *thinks* so (but it's just a stiff wind). That's why lab animals get nearly violent whenever a research assistant stimulates their amygdala.

The upshot is that the amygdala has a very short window of opportunity to wreak havoc—about twelve seconds, to be more exact. That's the approximate length of time of the "occipital spike," sort of a rush of awareness that stirs the amygdala's decision-making. It's the amygdala's warning siren, and it's the source of our psychological triggers that set off emotional outbursts.

When your brain is alerted by a new impulse or stimulus—like a car backfiring or a balloon popping—the occipital spike surges. The amygdala then dutifully surveys the landscape to see what's going on. This spike lasts twelve seconds and then, given that the stimulus doesn't repeat itself, turns off until the next emergency. The amygdala goes back to whatever it was doing before the spike.

These twelve seconds dictate our *external* reactions to whatever the amygdala is fussing about. And it's possible to control more extreme responses by recognizing when the spike happens and taking countermeasures to decompress the response, if indeed it was a "false alarm." This is especially helpful with people who get angry and are easily provoked by minor, almost irrelevant actions (remember, the amygdala goes nuts over *perceived* threats as well).

If one can restrain the occipital spike through some calming action—counting deep breaths, reciting the alphabet backward, saying a mantra, or even silently repeating a tongue-twister—then they can divert the amygdala until the spike fades. Remember, it only lasts twelve seconds or so. Others may form a mental picture of the spike and visualize it going back down. Whatever the effort, the key is to keep the thinking part of the brain occupied for as long as the amygdala needs until it goes back to its nap.

Psychological triggers are therefore tightly bound to our biology, and our brain chemistry provides those triggers with plenty of willing accomplices that let them build, persist, and go off. The fact that psychological triggers are part of our organic makeup can be irritating, but it should be of at least *some* consolation that they're a result of our natural descent from our forebears.

There is nothing wrong with this part of our biology, and indeed, it's the very thing that has allowed us to survive and thrive as the species we are today. Nevertheless, if we're not careful, we can let our fears control us completely—think social anxiety to the highest degree and every decision predicated on staying safe and secure. Being dictated by triggers to say the least!

Does Free Will Exist?

So with all these psychological triggers having so much power and authority over our brains and our reactions, is there even such a *thing* as free will? Why should we consider our actions anything other than pre-coded responses to external impulses? When I choose to do something drastic, am I *actually* choosing it, or am I being pushed and pulled into it by something I don't even realize?

As you might expect, philosophers have wrangled with the question of free will for ages. It's arguably their biggest moneymaker. In the days before brain research and science became widespread, free will was seen as the conduit for our moral code: we *chose* certain courses of action because they resounded with what we were taught society had to be. Therefore, if we wanted to perceive ourself as good people, we would choose positively; if we were corrupt in moral character, we would choose negatively.

Furthermore, we chose marital partners because they met our standards; we formed communities to live among those who shared our values. On an uglier note, we sometimes tried to force our will upon others in wars and invasions. Whatever the case, we believed we were doing the "right thing" voluntarily and deciding all on our own.

That argument was complicated when desire, perceived as involuntary, was identified as a motivator beyond human control. Now brain science—and its findings and resultant products, like this book—has muddied up the waters even more by suggesting our biological makeup could be the result of evolutionary forces we can't affect. How can we have free will when the amygdala makes us lose control and merely react for twelve frantic seconds?

Psychologists—who aren't and can't be philosophers—haven't been able to form a consensus on this question: do we have free will or not? *Why* do we do what we do, *especially* when so much of it is self-defeating and even pointless? Are we just rats continually pressing a lever that causes us to be shocked?

Sigmund Freud, the father of psychoanalysis (and also the originator of the concepts of the *ego*, *id*, and *superego*), and B.F. Skinner, the father of behaviorism, didn't necessarily have a lot of beliefs in common (Skinner, in fact, was downright resentful of Freud). But they shared the view that human behavior is highly subject to various experiences and conditions.

Freud focused primarily on unconscious influences on behavior (dreams, childhood, sexual impulses), whereas Skinner concentrated on direct environmental impact on behavior (rewards, social conditioning, education). So both had the conviction that humans don't have a real choice, but they conceived of it in quite different ways. Free will was, to them, an illusion that some used to congratulate themselves for not slapping other people indiscriminately.

Perhaps there are areas where we do have to make certain choices based on intellectual analysis and how our actions correspond to our beliefs. We *can* choose certain religions, political parties, associations, or movements (even if we're born into one, we can make the decision to join another one). There's a point where we come to a moral, intellectual understanding of issues, and we make choices that reflect that effort to understand.

But this doesn't apply to everything—or even most things. In fact, let's call intellectually independent choices made out of free will the exception rather than the rule. With all our respect and pondering of free will, there are still elements of our being that we can't control to the smallest detail. They're the instincts that our ancestors had to develop the hard way by burning their fingers in the fire, and they've commuted themselves into our present biology.

They might be simple fear, our subconscious, or the environment, but none of these are things we consciously perceive and acknowledge in our decisions. We are triggered day in and day out, and it's only when we can accept this that we can work against those triggers.

Controlling deep-rooted psychological triggers outright isn't possible, but being aware and remembering them can make them a lot more bearable and manageable. In this book, we'll take a deeper look at how these triggers get formed—starting with what's going on in our immediate surroundings.

Takeaways:

- What are psychological triggers? Put simply, they are what drive our behavior far more than we would care to admit or even think about. We are slaves to our impulses—and for most of us, this manifests in horribly negative ways.

- Triggers stem from evolutionary risk detection, which means that we have evolved to avoid pain and seek pleasure. We may not even realize what we are doing and may be unable to point out what pain and pleasure we are orienting ourselves around. Our impulses kept us alive in prior days but are wholly unsuited for the modern age.

- The best example of this phenomenon is phobias, which are irrational fears of benign harms—for instance, being afraid of heights, spiders, or deep water. Objectively, they are not directly harmful to you, but there's something primal, deep inside of us, that makes us react. What powers all of these triggers thus far? Fear and anxiety—possibly the most universal and predictable psychological trigger in the world.

Where fear exists, you can count on irrational behavior, because fear makes us want to act quickly, not intelligently or effectively.

- If psychological triggers are so commonplace and frequent, to what degree are we actually acting out of free will? Are we choosing our own lives, or are we just a complex set of impulses and influences? When you take into account fear, along with Freud's concept of the subconscious, with a dash of Skinner's reliance on the environment, it becomes clear that acting out of free will is the exception rather than the rule.

Chapter 2. Social Triggers

This chapter is about the influence of the people around us. The actions and words of others in our immediate and extended environments are powerful sources of psychological triggers. When you think about it, how could it be any other way? We first come into this world completely helpless and dependent immediately on other people, and our interactions with them last until the day we die.

We may think our minds operate independently of others, but humans are social animals at heart, and the desire to conform to the crowd is an innate and potent one. We're pack animals that don't stand a chance of surviving alone or in isolation. This leads us to take actions to be part of the group, and as you might expect, not all those actions are wise or sound decisions. If we think we are making a decision by ourselves, think again!

Peer pressure is the most obvious form of social influence, and it doesn't just happen during our formative childhood and adolescent years. The old trope "keeping up with the Joneses" is an example of how we experience social influence as adults. The motion of the people around us gradually becomes a huge part of how we experience the world and how we see ourselves fitting into it. It's not something we are conscious of, but social influence is a major player in our brains.

For example, consider a young family in which one of the partners has a reliable but modest income and rents a comfortable but cheap apartment in the suburbs. They might not live high on the hog, but they're not unhappy. But they might have longtime friends who are moving up the social ladder much more quickly than they are: they own their homes, they have newer and more expensive cars, they take exotic vacations, and they get neat stuff.

Now, none of their friends may be consciously pressuring them to step up in status, but that doesn't matter. The family still *feels* like they're behind. So they make a couple of purchases they're not financially ready for: a new house, a new car, expensive furniture, a trip to Europe. They run up their credit line. They don't have a lot left over for emergencies. They eventually put themselves into a pile of debt. And their friends are *still* moving up the ladder faster than they are. Before they know it, the breadwinner's lost their job, their income stream has stopped, and they have to declare bankruptcy.

The family wasn't unhappy before. They only thought they were unhappy and unsatisfied because of what their friends were doing and buying. And the family went to extreme measures to conform to their friends' wealth and status before they were ready. Curiously, this example demonstrates that social influence is not just on behavior—people can impact how you feel about yourself, about others, your beliefs, values and entire worldview.

That's how social influence affects us: it sets off triggers that convince us we need to be where everyone else is and that we need to take measures to get there even if they're dangerously risky. If not that, it alerts us to act to conform out of fear, social embarrassment, the threat of "losing face," or simple shame. And it's not just in terms of status or material wealth that our social surroundings pressure us. The pressure just triggers us into whichever way everyone else is leaning.

We're Independent, Right...?

If you walk into your new job and you find everyone wearing magenta shirts, you are probably going to find a magenta shirt as soon as you can for the next day, despite the fact that there is no dress code and no one has ever mentioned anything about magenta shirts. Something in your mind will tell you that you should be conforming to the people around you, even though there are no rules about it and the people you've asked haven't mentioned it, either.

We are heavily influenced by the people around us and the contexts we find ourselves in, to such a degree that free will might be just another factor influencing behavior, to be lumped in with our mood, the weather, and how hungry we are. If free will is a pleasant myth we like to believe in, then another myth is the one in which the single individual is the unit of agency and intention, deciding in a void what they want to do. Perhaps actions are carried out not so much on an individual basis but collectively, more as social and relational phenomena.

I want to cover three infamous, landmark studies that show just how little our actions are determined by free will and instead are decided by the social settings around us. These studies shed light on why we feel compelled to wear a magenta shirt even if there is no dress code and why people tend to act against their own interests or values.

The first study that digs deep into the concept of dubious free will is the *Asch conformity experiment*, and many people are familiar with its findings precisely because they so directly undermine our assumption that human beings can act alone and purely on their own free will.

This study was conducted by Solomon Asch of Swarthmore College in the 1950s and broadly demonstrated the compulsion to conform and "fit in" even when doing so goes against our best instincts and interests.

The study was relatively simply and asked participants to engage in a vision test. In each run of the study, there was only one subject, and the rest of the people present were Asch's confederates. They would attempt to influence the true participant to conform and act against their free will.

The participant sat around a table with seven confederates and was asked two questions:

1. Which line was the longest in Exhibit 2?
2. Which line from Exhibit 2 matches the line from Exhibit 1?

Below is what the participants saw and made their judgment on. When participants were asked this question alone, through writing, or without confederates who would provide a range of answers, they consistently answered in the exact same way: obviously, Line C and Line A, respectively.

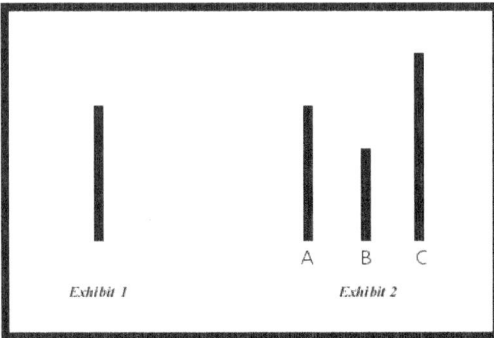

Exhibit 1   Exhibit 2

However, when confederates were present and provided incorrect answers, what followed was surprising.

When the true participant was surrounded by confederates who gave incorrect answers, such as stating that Line C was equal to Exhibit 1 or that Line B was the longest in Exhibit 2, they also conformed their answers to be stunningly incorrect based on the social pressures of the people around them. Over one-third of the true participants gave an obviously wrong answer, presumably because of the influence of peer pressure and the general feeling of "What could I be missing that everyone else is seeing?"

This feeling of confusion and wanting to avoid appearing stupid can cause someone to conform to something obviously wrong, which will actually make them appear stupid because they were trying to avoid that very thing. Asch successfully displayed that people, whether they believe it or not, wish to blend in with their peers and their environment so they don't stick out.

People don't want to commit a social faux pas, so whether they thought the line was truly the same length or not, they made it seem like they did. Follow-ups to Asch's experiment showed that this effect increased when there were more confederates present. If there were one or two confederates who gave incorrect answers, the effects were small, but if there were more than two, then people seemed to feel a significantly greater sense of peer pressure.

It seems there is comfort in numbers—if three people see something a certain way, then I might be the one missing something, but if only one person disagrees with me, then they are equally as likely as me to be missing something.

Asch commented, "The tendency to conformity in our society is so strong that reasonably intelligent and well-meaning young people are willing to call white black." He had the opportunity to ask participants after the experiment whether they actually believed their altered stances, and most did not and simply wanted to go along with the group because they did not want to be thought of as "peculiar." Others thought the group's judgment was actually correct and felt their new answer to be correct as well.

These two approaches represent the two main reasons people appeared to conform and act against their own free will. First, they wanted to be liked by the group and not seen as a "peculiar" outsider—this is called a normative influence. They wanted to fit in and be viewed as comparable to the group. Second, they conformed because they thought their information was faulty, and they wanted to use the group's judgment instead of their own. This is called an informational influence, where they doubted their own instincts and assumed others had more and better information than they did. You can easily imagine how these two tendencies play out in our daily lives.

In either case, people's sense of free will is subverted by emotional reactions to what other people are doing. You can say that you chose to go along with other people's answers consciously, but in fact, it wasn't what you truly wanted to do.

This is how we end up wearing magenta shirts far more often than we think we should. If you work in an office full of magenta shirt wearers, you might start with buying only one, but by the end of a year, you'll probably have a closet full of magenta shirts just because it seems like the right thing to do to fit in. You want acceptance from the group to not appear "peculiar," and you feel there's a reason magenta is so prevalent, one you don't quite know yet.

It might not be a surprise that we take cues on how to behave and think from other people, especially if it's a situation that is foreign to us. For instance, if you show up at a fancy ball, you would look to how other people bow, stand, and interact so you can calibrate your own behavior. Where this takes a deviation into subverting free will is where you go directly against what you know to be true just to conform. Asch's experiment was one instance where a clearly correct answer was passed over, showing the true power of peer pressure and social influence.

The psychological implications of Asch's experiment may not be groundbreaking—we are all afraid of judgment, but the degree to which we strive to avoid it is huge and can be said to make us followers in a negative way.

Many people may like to think that they themselves would never behave this way, but the fact remains that it's human nature to want to belong, and to do this, we often allow the group to make decisions for us instead of relying on our own judgment. Even if you derive much of your identity from being a loner or an independent outsider, at some point there will be *some* group that you will strive to identify with. Have you ever noticed that those who identify as rebels nevertheless tend to wear their own "uniform" and keep up with their own version of the "Joneses"?

The next study was infamous for how it supposedly shed light onto humanity's dark side. Building on the theme of free will, it showed how mankind's best intentions and values could be threatened—or perhaps even explain how good men and women have behaved with so much depravity in historical atrocities like the Holocaust.

Stanley Milgram's experiment chronicled in his 1963 paper "Obedience to Authority: An Experimental View" is one of the most important and famous psychological experiments ever conducted. And for our purposes, it demonstrates how we become slaves to authority and generally don't act in accordance to our individual values when ordered to do something under the guise of a duty. In more recent times, remembering the conclusions of Milgram's experiment can explain atrocities as unthinkable as torture of prisoners of war, or even the genocide that was allowed to occur during World War II.

People aren't inherently evil and don't necessarily use their free will to inflict such harm. Instead, Milgram showed us another explanation as to why people can act in horrific ways while still remaining very human at heart. His findings can serve as a general lesson on why people who have done dark things aren't different from you or me.

Milgram began his research at Yale University in the 1960s with the initial impetus of studying the psychology of genocide. He began to theorize that people who participated in genocide weren't necessarily evil, twisted, or even different from those who *didn't* commit genocide but that it was rather a reflection of authority, orders, and the perception of a lack of accountability. In other words, if you were just being told what to do and you were conditioned to follow orders without question, there was a pretty good chance you would be able to carry out those orders—no matter what they were.

After all, that is the reason soldiers go through boot camp and are berated endlessly by drill instructors—it is a process designed to promote obedience and conformity, even in the worst conditions that combat will present. However, Milgram's experiment showed it wasn't only trained soldiers who could fall victim to such blind obedience and have their free will taken away from them. Haven't we all bowed to authority throughout life, without much of a second thought?

To examine these behaviors more closely, Milgram built a "shock machine" that looked like a device that would be used to dole out torture, but in reality, it did nothing and was mostly a series of lights and dials. This would be his tool for exposing human nature.

His experiment worked on the premise that the participant was administering a memory test to someone in another room, and if the unseen person made a mistake on the test, the participant was given the instruction from a man in a white lab coat to punish them with electric shocks stemming from the "shock machine."

The shocks would escalate in intensity based on how many wrong answers were given. Before the start of the experiment, the participant was given a 45-volt electric shock that was attached to the shock machine. Forty-five volts was where the shocks would begin and then increase in 15-volt increments with each mistake. The shock machine went up to 450 volts, which also had a warning label reading "Danger: Severe Shock" next to it, and the final two switches were also labeled "XXX."

Of course, no shocks were really given at all. The unseen test-taker was actually an actor who followed a script of getting the vast majority of the questions incorrect. As the participant administered shocks, goaded on and encouraged by the man in the white lab coat, the actor would cry out loudly and begin to express pain and anguish, begging them to stop and then eventually falling completely silent.

Despite this, pushed on by the man in the white lab coat, a full 62 percent of participants administered the electrical shocks up to the highest level, which included the "XXX" and "Danger" levels. Milgram only allowed the man in the white lab coat to encourage with neutral and relatively benign statements such as "Please continue" and "It is absolutely essential that you continue."

In other words, the participants weren't coerced within an inch of their lives to, in their perception, shock someone to unconsciousness or death! There was no proverbial gun to anybody's head. Yet 62 percent reached the 450-volt limit, and none of the subjects stopped before reaching 300 volts. At 315 volts, the unseen actors went silent. The participants weren't being forced to do this and weren't being yelled at or threatened. How could these shocking results have occurred?

Are people just callous and have little regard for human life and suffering outside of their own? That can't be true—and indeed many of us recoil at the results, convinced that *we* would never behave this way. No, we're not evil. What's more likely to be true is how persuasive the perception of authority can be in subverting our free will. We will act against our wishes if we sense that we are being ordered to by someone who has power over us, no matter how arbitrary.

This obedience to authority and sense of deference can even push us to electrocute an innocent person to implied death. Suddenly, things such as genocide, the Holocaust, and torturing prisoners of war don't seem so far-fetched. We like to think we have hard limits on what we could inflict on others, but the results of Milgram's experiments showed otherwise—our free will was completely bypassed because of a simple display of authority.

Milgram noted other factors in the study participants' behavior might include the feeling that, because there was an authority figure, they would hold no accountability and be able to say, "Well, he told me to!"

When the participants were reminded they held responsibility for their actions, almost none of them wanted to continue participating in the experiment, and many even refused to continue if the man in the white lab coat didn't take explicit responsibility.

Additionally, it was an unseen victim they had never met before, so there was a degree of separation and dehumanization that allowed actions to go further. Either way, these factors tell us something rather unflattering about human nature and how our free will really plays out in the real world, under pressure.

In the end, a normal person was shown to have followed orders given by another ordinary person in a white lab coat with a semblance of authority, which culminated in killing another person. It was quite the discovery in terms of what drives and motivates people. It was a very powerful piece of evidence that our free will is subject to all manners of delusion and influence.

Finally, the infamous Stanford prison experiment was conducted on the campus of Stanford University by prominent psychologist Philip Zimbardo in 1973, and he wanted to examine a few hypotheses. Even if you've never heard of this experiment before, it's telling that you can probably imagine the outcome already.

Similar to the Milgram shock experiments, Zimbardo wanted to test how the presence of roles of authority would drive people to do things drastically out of their nature and into an area some might call sadistic. He specifically wanted to investigate whether the brutality that was being reported in prisons throughout the nation was because the prisons had a tendency to attract sadistic people, or because of the inherent power differential between guards and prisoners.

Zimbardo found participants and randomly assigned them the role of prisoner or prison guard in a simulated jail complex built on the university campus. He theorized that if they all acted in nonaggressive ways, then abuse was happening in prison institutions because of the inherent bad actors and biased population—not because of the toxic environment. If the participants acted the same as guards and prisoners did in real prisons, that would be an argument for the corrupting influence of the prison environment itself.

Both groups of participants were told to adhere to their roles as closely as possible, though it quickly became clear the guards did this far more zealously than the prisoners. The guards wore sunglasses to avoid making eye contact, they punished prisoners who misbehaved by assigning them to solitary confinement cells, and they only referred to prisoners by their identification numbers instead of their names. In addition, the prisoners were stripped naked, showered in front of each other, and only given prison clothes. This was as close to prison environment as was possible.

This next part was critical: the guards were given free rein to do whatever they felt was necessary to maintain a functional prison cell, maintain order, and maintain respect from the prisoners. There was no physical violence allowed, but there were certainly many other ways bad behavior began to leak out. For instance, the guards would wake up the prisoners at 2:30 in the morning just because they wanted to show control and dominance. Forced push-ups until collapse was not uncommon as a form of punishment and general breaking of the spirit.

The guards embraced their roles, which caused the prisoners to embrace theirs. They began to act exactly like prisoners act in real prisons by ganging up against other prisoners, trying to curry favor with the guards, and taking the rules very seriously. One prisoner went on a hunger strike to try to gain better treatment for the prisoners, but his cohorts didn't rally behind him; rather, they viewed him as a troublemaker who was going to cause them problems if he didn't stop.

Very quickly, the treatment of the prisoners by the guards became worse and spiraled into near-abuse. Toilet facilities became a privilege instead of a basic human right, with access to the bathroom being frequently denied, and the inmates often had to clean the facilities with their bare hands. Prisoners were stripped naked and subjected to sexual humiliation.

These were normal people put into roles with a huge power differential. Despite how morally good many of the guards felt they were, the majority didn't object to this treatment of the prisoners, and Zimbardo estimated one-third of the guards began to spiral into extremely sadistic behavior and thought patterns. Free will be damned— people began to play the roles they were assigned. People may not be inherently evil or sadistic, but when put into powerful positions over people that are sufficiently dehumanized, they tend to act in predictable ways.

The Stanford prison experiment was slated to run for fourteen days, but Zimbardo felt it had to end by the sixth day. The behavior was growing out of control. People began to identify with their roles in horrifying and negative ways. The guards took the modicum of power they had and expanded it as much as possible, while the prisoners became more dejected over time. While prison guards in a vacuum may be as sensitive and courteous as the rest of us, the roles they inhabit take a toll on how they view others.

The guards egged each other on, and their behavior kept degrading because of a mob mentality. Zimbardo had neatly answered his question of whether it was situational or personal factors that contributed to the abuse rampant in the country's prison systems. When people are put into specific roles, they will live up to that role, plain and simple. It doesn't necessarily matter what someone's normal temperament is. People's free will is again undermined or pushed to the side in order to fulfill the duties of a role, to blend in, and to meet others' expectations.

The scientists of these three experiments prove the simple fact that when it comes to the actions we take, who we think we are doesn't matter. How we wish to present ourselves to the world doesn't matter. Even our worldview, values, and opinions don't matter.

What matters more in determining how we will act are the people around us. Our typical definition of free will is one that allows us to dictate the path we force through life. Unfortunately, these three experiments show us that what we do doesn't always match up with our intentions.

Of course, we can't just isolate ourselves from strangers and loved ones alike in our quest to avoid psychological triggers and think freely. Relationships are important. Loneliness isn't just depressing; it's also harmful. But our attachment to family and friends eventually results in their having a measure of influence in our minds, and our influence in theirs. That can be good, but it can also be not good. Asch, Milgram, and Zimbardo would agree with the latter.

The Consuming Psychology of Crowds

In the above experiments, external influences were seen to impact the individual's behavior—this is the "peer pressure" idea, or the effects we see when those around us have the power to sway us one way or another. But what about larger groups of people? What do we know about the behavior of large groups?

We can take what we learn from the above experiments in individual behavior and ask how they apply to the actions of groups of people—i.e. the psychology of crowds. Several prominent theories attempt to explain why it is that crowds of people often seem to follow their own laws, or act in ways that the individuals making up the crowd would never resort to if they were alone.

It's only recently that psychologists have tended to consider the individual the unit of interest. Conversely, early 19th-century psychology was more interested in group behavior, and psychologist Gustavo Le Bon had a theory about crowds that was based on what he called, perhaps unkindly, "mob psychology."

Le Bon painted a picture of crowd behavior as largely irrational and even somewhat dangerous, but the idea that crowds could behave in unconscious or uncontrolled ways has been tempered somewhat in recent years. Le Bon was interested in why people form riots or get into group panics, how they behave when they're in an audience, how they act when in a mass social movement, a march, or even just in public, as well as why people gossip or start rumors.

In Le Bon's time, it was not uncommon to assume the cause of social upheavals, political unrest, and spontaneous riots was purely psychological, and down to some moral failing of a person, a whole class of people, or even of humankind as a whole. Though there have been many documented cases of spontaneous irrational and even dangerous action that later seemed senseless, there are just as many examples of crowds behaving toward a unified end because of shared political and social sentiment.

Today, research is showing that group human behavior is a lot more mindful, nuanced and intelligent than Le Bon believed, and that the results found in the Asch and Milgram experiments may not play out quite as simply in real life, non-experimental conditions. If you were to ask any participating member of the historic Stonewall riots *why* they had rioted, for example, they would not have given you a response in line with Le Bon's theory—but they might have spoken at length about the history and politics of the LGBT movement at the time, and how their action was not a random outburst of repressed drives but a deliberate retaliation against violence and discrimination.

At the heart of Le Bon's theory was the idea that group behavior is always emotionally determined. He believed that crowds formed and acted according to shared feelings, for example of fear or anger, which then served as a bond to tie the group members together. This is frequently observed in riot and crowd behavior, especially the more spontaneous kind.

In a crowd, however, emotions are further stirred up because people are focusing on them so intently—it's as though the words, symbols, body language and general tone of the crowd itself froths up strong feelings. This is why chanted slogans, powerful imagery and emotive language are used so effectively in crowds.

Once emotionally activated, a crowd can be led and even manipulated. The trouble, according to Le Bon and other theorists, is that this flood of emotion dampens any critical thinking, independent thought or calm, rational analysis. Le Bon claimed that these instincts to emote are always inside a person, but we're usually able to keep a lid on them. In a crowd, however, something happens to loosen this normal restraint, and free will takes a back seat.

The man in the crowd "possesses the spontaneity, the violence, the ferocity and also the enthusiasm and heroism of primitive beings," said Le Bon. A "group mind" seems to take over as the individual mind dissolves—and the group mind may think and behave very differently from the individuals in the group, were they to be isolated. In other words, the group is not merely the sum of its parts; it takes on an entirely new character distinct from that of its members.

Le Bon saw the man in the crowd as excited and essentially hypnotized toward one single, emotional object. Though there are virtues to this kind of energy, the emphasis was often on the *irrationality* of groups— something you might have witnessed yourself if you've been to a sports game, a political rally, a protest or a bar fight.

How does a rational person get into this state? One key feature is anonymity. When you feel personally invisible, it's easier to act without responsibility, and detach yourself from your individual morality. Another feature is the "contagion" idea— the theory that behavior spreads in a group like a virus, causing people to mimic and mirror one another. This wouldn't be possible without the third feature: suggestibility.

The psychologist William McDougall was also interested in the factors that allow ordinarily smart, kind and calm people to behave in completely uncharacteristic ways. He, too, identified the heightening of emotion together with the dampening of rational thoughts as key to crowd behavior. He thought that the intensification of strong emotions was due to "primitive sympathetic response," i.e. our human ability to match the emotional state of those around us. And the more people we observe expressing a particular emotion, the greater the chance we end up feeling similarly.

People end up mutually intensifying shared emotions, and their resistance or ability to push back is weakened. Like Le Bon, McDougall had plenty of unflattering things to say about people in crowds: that they were fickle, impulsive, extreme, coarse, overly suggestible and emotional, careless, lacking self-consciousness and self-respect, irresponsible, easily manipulated... and basically incredibly stupid.

It's no surprise that Freud, who was similarly unimpressed by irrational, unconscious or overly emotional behavior, had something to say about crowd dynamics, too. Freud wrote an essay titled *Group Psychology and Analysis of Ego*, where he pointed to what he believed kept a group together: a shared emotional connection.

Freud and several other theorists believed that people behaved as they did in groups in order to release latent instincts and desires. It's as though in a crowd, the well-behaved, restraining superego is given permission to relax and the more primitive impulses of the ego and id can come to the fore. The crowd is essentially an excuse to give free rein to drives that are ordinarily not unleashed.

Freud's theory, however, is not really supported by observational evidence. It's simply not true that all crowds are acting out because of repressed instincts—and there's a lot to crowd behavior that isn't adequately explained by this drive-focused theory.

If the theories of Freud, Le Bon and McDougall seem a little misanthropic to you, you're not the only one. Later psychologist F. H. Allport believed that crowds actually served an important social function, and formed simply as a natural response to a shared stimulus. The sociologist Ralf Turner similarly claimed that crowds are not in fact a chaotic free-for-all, but possess their own social norms and mutually agreed upon, sanctioned behavior. If you've been to a well-organized march or, well, a very good party, you might agree with this observation. Nevertheless, the way people (sometimes) behave in crowds can give us some important insights into the often hidden, unacknowledged and uncontrolled causes of our behavior.

Even though these various theories offer quite different explanations for crowd behavior, they do show that it likely comes down to a complex mix of all these factors, including unconscious drives, suggestibility, anonymity and heightened emotion. A situation where all these factors are strongly present may make a crowd or riot more likely to develop, and when it does, it may well be of the kind that Le Bon and Freud call "primitive."

In keeping with this book's general theme, we can understand all these factors that influence crowds as psychological triggers that drive our behavior. Though we all like to think that we are always operating under our own individual, free will and are 100 percent rational, the truth is more likely that we are swayed by the emotions and behaviors of others.

But what if people do behave completely irrationally, and even worse, *have no idea* that they are doing so? In a crowd or mob, it's easy to see how a single leader or external manipulation can sway a group this way or that. But in the next section we'll see that sometimes, we are perfectly capable of deceiving and manipulating ourselves—and being left none the wiser.

Clever Hans and the Ideomotor Effect

The final way that a lack of free will derives from our peculiar brains is the *ideomotor effect.* This phenomenon occurs when our unconscious minds transform our expectations into reality through involuntary physical reactions; we do it to ourselves, other people do it to us, and this all results in a confusing carousel wheel where it's impossible to determine the true cause or reason for an act. One thing is for sure, though—it's not our conscious choice.

The emphasis here is on the words "unconscious" and "involuntary." Because we don't know we're causing the actions and we cannot control them, the results can be surprising—for others and for ourselves—and can even trick us into thinking there's magic or supernatural forces at work. As one might expect, there is another, more logical explanation.

Some examples will explain clearly what this effect is—you may even recognize how it may have played a role in your own life once or twice. Perhaps the most famous example of the ideomotor effect at work is the story of Clever Hans. Clever Hans was a horse that many believed could perform intellectual tasks such as telling time and doing basic math, for example.

During the early 1900s, the horse's owner Wilhelm von Osten made Hans somewhat of a celebrity by carting him around Germany and showcasing his "talents" to the public. The performance would go something like this: Osten would ask the horse to calculate the sum of five plus three, and Clever Hans would tap his hoof eight times. Of course, the crowd would go wild, and von Osten would praise the horse for his superior intellect.

Not everyone believed Clever Hans was so smart, though. The German Board of Education along with psychologists Carl Stumpf and Oskar Pfungst decided to get to the bottom of the horse's unusual behavior. They designed an experiment to determine if the horse could perform the same tasks under different circumstances. After testing Hans under many different conditions, they discovered that he answered correctly only when he could see his prompter and only when the prompter knew the answer to the question being asked.

In other words, Hans couldn't add two plus two, but when asked by someone who could, he would tap four times, provided he could see the questioner. The researchers further surmised that the questioner would change their body language and posture as the horse was tapping out the answer.

This altered stance occurred in unconscious anticipation of Hans arriving at the correct answer. The questioner would change their stance again upon the arrival of the final tap, providing a visual cue for Hans to stop. The questioner hoped Hans would answer correctly, which caused them to behave as if he would, and so he did. This can be a purposeful behavior, but it can also happen entirely unconsciously, meaning the questioner may well believe the act themselves.

Who is exercising free will in this situation? None of the human parties, anyway. The intention may match the result, but it's a choice that is not independently made.

The ideomotor effect is similar to a self-fulfilling prophecy. You've probably heard Henry Ford's famous quote, "If you think you can or if you think you can't, you're right." It's become a popular motivational saying used to encourage people to think positively so that their positive thoughts bring about positive behaviors. It may sound overly simplistic, but it actually works. (Try it!)

When you genuinely believe you can do something, you're actually more likely to achieve the goal. The reverse is true, too. When you doubt your abilities, your abilities are automatically compromised. Keep telling yourself you'll never get a promotion at work, for instance, and you likely never will. Self-fulfilling prophecies occur (and frequently!) because thoughts are powerful things that can indeed affect reality.

A self-fulfilling prophecy is a lot like thinking yourself into a result, good or bad. You make a prediction—or "prophecy"—about what you think is likely to happen and begin acting as if your prediction has already occurred, which in turn causes it to actually happen.

For instance, consider bachelor Ted who agrees to go out on a date with Claire, a woman he believes to be way out of his league. He tells himself the date will be a disaster because Claire will immediately recognize that he's not good enough for her. He worries about this prediction all the way to the bar, and by the time he gets there, he's sweating bullets. He opens his mouth to greet her, and no words come out. He completely freezes, which weirds Claire out, setting the disastrous tone for the rest of the evening.

Would it have gone differently had Ted never predicted a catastrophic first date in the first place? Absolutely!

The ideomotor effect is also similar to *confirmation bias*, a cognitive tendency to recall or search for information that confirms something you already believe to be true. For example, if you believe everyone at your job hates you, you'll look for instances in which coworkers respond sharply to you or supervisors criticize your work. Mentally, you'll prove your theory— at least to yourself—that no one likes you. Everyone is susceptible to confirmation bias—even scientists—and the more powerful the belief, the more likely it is that confirmation bias will take hold.

Where the ideomotor effect differs from cognitive phenomena like self-fulfilling prophecies and confirmation bias is in its ability to cause an immediate physical reaction in addition to a cognitive one. The idea that an unconscious thought can trigger an involuntary reaction may seem disturbing, but it happens all the time. Once you start looking, you may see surprising examples of this all around you—and all the while with people thinking their free will is calling the shots!

The ideomotor effect is responsible for many people's staunch belief in Ouija boards, for example. People who have used these boards may swear the planchette is moving on its own when really the participant is unconsciously moving it via the ideomotor effect in order to fulfill their subconscious expectations. It's important to note that these expectations (and of course the resulting muscular movements) are not voluntary, and the participants don't know they're causing the movement.

Thus, when asked, they'll report that the planchette was moving itself (or was moved by a spirit or ghost). So while Ouija boards aren't proof that we can communicate with the dead, they are proof that our unconscious thoughts and expectations are much more powerful than we may have ever realized! Add this to the effects of social pressure and the phenomena discovered in the Asch experiments, and you'll soon see how even rational, skeptical people can start to believe in the unbelievable.

Dowsing rods work in a similar way. For centuries, pseudoscientists have claimed to be able to use rods of varying types to locate things like oil, precious metals, and groundwater. Though they claim to have some sort of divine power, what they're really experiencing is another unintended consequence of the ideomotor effect.

Put simply, their bodies are reacting involuntarily to the expectations in their minds regarding where something might be located, causing a muscle twitch that then causes the rod to point in a particular direction. Real science has repeatedly proven the results of dowsing to be unreliable.

The ideomotor effect isn't just the stuff of horror movies and variety shows, though. It has had many other real-world manifestations, and not all of them have been innocent. On the contrary, some have had heart-breaking and even life-ending consequences.

In the case of facilitated communication, loved ones of those suffering from conditions such as retardation or cerebral palsy that prohibit them from speaking have been fooled into thinking these patients can communicate with them by signaling a facilitator who then types on a keyboard.

Despite continual warnings from the American Psychological Association (APA) that facilitated communication has no scientific basis, many people still hold on to false hope that their debilitated friends and family members are really communicating with them through some medium. In many cases, people are grateful to the facilitators at first for helping them speak with the person they love. Imagine their despair, though, when they eventually find out that it was nothing but a farce.

Then there's the case of Brit Jim McCormick, who was convicted of fraud in 2013 for selling fake bomb detectors to countries around the world, including Iraq, Syria, and Mexico. He claimed the devices could detect bombs, even if they were very far away or buried underground. As it turns out, the gadgets did nothing at all, except act as a catalyst for the ideomotor effect. It is said that hundreds of lives were lost because of the ruse.

Remember, though, in many cases—maybe even most cases—those who succeed in deceiving others with the ideomotor effect do so unwittingly and never realize the truth behind their antics. They effectively deceived others only because they so thoroughly deceived themselves, first.

For instance, facilitators who claim to help invalids communicate think they're helping both the patient and his or her loved ones. They're genuinely not trying to trick anyone; they're simply naïve. Often, they continue to believe their own "lie" even after being proven wrong by reputable scientists over and over again.

Even Wilhelm von Osten had nothing to gain by making Hans a show pony; he never charged a dime for the horse's performances. These aren't bad people trying to pull the wool over the world's eyes. They're just human beings who happen to have fallen victim to the ideomotor effect. Some people may find it disconcerting to discover just how convincing the brain can be at deception.

After all, look how foolish von Osten seems in retrospect to believe a horse could do math! And what about the spectators? How could all of those people collectively believe in something that could clearly never happen? Scary, right? There is a silver lining, though. When one is aware of how the brain operates, he or she becomes less susceptible to its trickery.

In fact, the only way to outsmart the brain is simply not to take its conclusion at face value. Weighing subjective perceptions against cold, hard facts and concrete data is the only way to avoid being duped by our own minds and to see things with any semblance of clarity. We're not always wrong, of course, but knowing all the ways we can be can make these strange blunders less likely to occur.

There you have it—the ideomotor effect in action. Free will is our conscious and unfiltered intention set into action. Whether it exists or not is still a complicated question, but as this chapter demonstrates, it can certainly be compromised, interfered with and overpowered in many ways.

Here, we can see that our unconscious can easily take control in ways we have zero awareness of. Whatever choice you think you are making independently is only a compendium of social and unconscious factors.

Inoculation Theory

There is a way to battle social pressure, though: inoculation theory. The only obvious way to defend against the pressure from others and even from your own irrational unconscious is to be aware of what is going on in the first place. This awareness can then guide you to be prepared in the face of external persuasion. Though it's not always 100 percent certain that you can fend off such persuasion, you are still in a better position than if you had gone along with things completely unawares.

This philosophy helps us reinforce the positions and convictions that are most important to us and repel others' efforts to sway us. Inoculation of your point of view is a central part of being able to reject the aggressive assertions of other people, especially those who are skilled at presenting strong arguments. The idea behind inoculation theory is to expose and defy the parts of those arguments that aren't quite as powerful. In other words, you prevent the influence of a certain big idea by showing exactly what it's made of, bit by bit, and how it's intended to work on you.

Think of it this way: "inoculation" is somewhat synonymous with "immunization," which is the medical act of injecting a weak strain of virus into one's bloodstream so it can build up resistance to stronger strains. The body gets to know this weak virus and what it looks like. So when it's exposed to a stronger virus—which you can picture as being made up of several smaller viruses—it knows how to resist it.

Similarly, inoculation theory says that exposure to lighter or lower-impact aspects or lines of thought of arguments helps shore up our psychological immunity to those effects.

For example, say you're dealing with a salesman who's trying to get you to buy something you don't need. It doesn't matter what it is—a vacuum cleaner, a time-share condo, antivirus software, whatever. It's his job to make a very strong, very persuasive pitch to you. He's going to try and convince you that your life to this point has been lacking because you didn't have this product and that the only way you can go forward in your life is if you finally get it.

Now, this product might actually be of good quality. But that also doesn't matter. What matters is that he's trying to persuade you into buying it right this instant and you don't want to. And he's using tactics that every salesman is supposed to use: he's being aggressive, he's acting sympathetic to your problems, and he's trying to convince you that if you don't get this product as soon as possible things are going to get very bad very quickly.

Suppose you experienced the same types of tactics in smaller doses the day before with a similar salesman—your prior exposure to the strategies he's using has *inoculated* you against their effectiveness. He's trying to get you to think only about the product he's selling. You're thinking about *how* he's trying to sell you the product: the little psychological tricks he's using. Too bad he doesn't know you've had practice withstanding them, which allows you to escape their impact and think more freely.

Will that get rid of the salesman? Maybe. Maybe not. But that's not what you're really trying to do—you're only trying to *resist his influence*. You're doing that by picking apart his methods and exposing them for what they are. In doing so, you've reinforced your own resistance to them—in other words, you've become inoculated to his efforts.

To defend against being swayed or persuaded, you should get as familiar as possible with all possible angles a persuader might try and throw at you—and maybe even ones they haven't thought up yet. You can think of all their arguments, emotional pleas, sneaky tactics, and pains you will avoid and the pleasures you will enjoy from listening to them.

If you want to defend against the stronger arguments in favor of a reprehensible belief—say, the superiority of navel oranges to other oranges (or something even more provocative)—you'd familiarize yourself with every possible argument. Everyone's going to tell you navel oranges taste better and don't have seeds, so there's no point in going over that argument any more than you already have. But then someone might throw a curveball, saying that navel oranges are superior because they originated in Southern California. You could counter that with the truth: they were originally found in Brazil in the early 1800s as a mutant product of orange trees. So the entire basis of that argument is wrong. You'd only know that fact if you really probed deeply into the history of navel oranges.

Of course, that topic is inane unless for some reason you're a hardliner on oranges. But it's simple enough to form the basis of your approach toward topics with more import and potential offense. It shows the basic plan of how to resist influence that could cause irrational behavior. (Besides, navel oranges *are* better.)

The people around us make us act in ways we can't predict, sometimes because of their simple presence. Can we control this? Not unless you wish to become a social pariah. Therefore, we must learn to adopt independent thinking habits that steer us into rational thinking when it might not be the path of least resistance.

Takeaways:

- The people around us aren't just sources of companionship—they are one of the most powerful sources of influence and psychological triggers! It may not be conscious, and it may not even be peer pressure, but we almost never make decisions in a social vacuum, and this often has negative consequences. We are pressured to conform, we bend to displays of authority, and we fulfill the roles and labels we are given.

- Three seminal psychological studies showed how susceptible we are to social influence: the Asch conformity study, the Milgram shock study, and the Stanford prison experiment. How can we truly claim to be acting out of free will when shocking evidence exists otherwise?

- Theorists like Le Bon, McDougall and Freud saw crowd behavior as a powerful psychological trigger. Their theories characterized group behavior as irrational, emotionally driven, "primitive" and a means to release latent unconscious desires. More modern theorists such as Allport, however, concede that crowd behavior can actually serve a social function.

- The ideomotor effect suggests that people can unconsciously and involuntarily behave in ways so as to bring about expected or anticipated results—for example, subtly moving the Ouija board planchette themselves but sincerely believing that someone else (or a spirit!) moved it. There is no deception—only unconscious action. This shows us how easy it is for us to convince ourselves of something we want to be true.

- Perhaps we can't defend our free will very well, but at the very least we can learn a couple of habits to get better at thinking for ourselves. The first of these is learning to say no. This is tough for multiple reasons, but the solutions are plentiful. Start to say "I don't" versus "I can't," consider your beliefs about refusing people, resist the crucial moment of tension, and keep your thought process as nonpersonal as possible.

- The second habit to cultivate to think more rationally in the presence of others is to become an interrogator—that is, to ask questions about the source and the motives and to play devil's advocate to glean more information for yourself, and to stall while giving your rational mind time to overcome instinct.

- Inoculation theory is where you start to resist people's influences by exposing yourself to their arguments, specifically the weak parts, as much as possible beforehand. Once you can inoculate yourself against these persuasive angles and become adjusted to their impact and power, you can think more freely and avoid irrational decisions coming from people around you.

Chapter 3. The Emotions that Run Our Lives

The most common psychological triggers occur when our emotions seize command over us, whether positive or negative. For our purposes, feel free to include fear in that category.

Humans' ability to feel emotions differentiates us from many other creatures, but it also exposes us to illogical thought and behavior and the occasional craziness when we get too carried away. Emotions add color and depth to life; they give life poignancy and meaning; they infuse our values and dreams with nuance and tell us who we are—but they can also lead us astray, if we don't properly understand how to navigate them.

Emotions are intense experiences. They're the *first* source of information we receive about a given event or situation. They are unfiltered and immediate—which means they are, by definition, antithetical to rational thought. Emotions often feel instinctual and embodied, almost irresistible and even primal. Emotions arrive without much warning, rearrange our stable existences, and often get out of hand before we can shake ourselves back to rationality.

For instance, two extra-potent emotions that probably drive us more than any others are love and fear. We've covered fear a bit already in the previous chapter, but you can argue that *every* action or response is driven by one of those two if you think hard enough. Even more practical decisions could theoretically be traced back to love or fear. We buckle up our kids in the car because we love them and we fear the effects an accident can have on them. That's a practical move motivated by love and fear.

As for irrational? Remember when we talked about the fears of social anxiety and the life that creates? Those are just the beginning of how intense emotional arousal can cause us to literally lose our minds and simply act without thinking.

We're not talking about just *having* those emotions and the choices they encourage, though. We're talking about the high states of arousal to which those emotions can lead. Certainly, all of us have some experience with the results of these two emotions wreaking havoc. We've all known times when romantic love turned us (or someone we know) into stark, raving lunatics.

When there's potential for a romance and a perceived mutual interest from someone else, it suspends rationality in a big way. We're willing to let go of logic because love makes us feel good, and our pleasure center's job is to make sure we *keep* feeling good. We're more approachable and friendly. We take mental vacations from realistic or negative aspects of existence because we're feeling new excitement. Everywhere we go is the happiest place on Earth.

But it can turn into something sordid real quick. If you don't hear from the object of your affections for a period of time, you might ruminate as to why that happens. You think the other person might be losing interest. Your gut absorbs the punch. You begin to imagine worst-case scenarios: "Are they cheating? Were they just leading me on the whole time? Maybe I should phone them. Although they haven't answered my last couple of calls, I'll just keep calling every ten minutes until they pick up."

And *that* doesn't work, so you start to go a little loopy. You go to the address where they live. You knock on their door. They're not there. You experience intense anxiety. That turns into anger, and the next thing you know, you're pounding on their door. You're racing with rage and disappointment. You howl and cry. The situations you imagine get more and more lurid, and your assessments of your partner's character get more and more negative. You cast off any notion of just acting normally because you can't think about doing anything else but obsessing over and over. Next thing you know, you're in a holding cell because you sprayed graffiti on their door and the neighbors called the police.

This example might seem extreme, but that's because your rational mind is reading it and it sounds ridiculous. In reality, this situation can go (and has gone) into very dark, dangerous, and violent territory. That's because the emotional arousal we get from love overtakes all sensibility and sets off a virtual fireworks display full of psychological triggers. Heightened states rob us of our logic, as we begin to focus only on what will either prolong a happy emotional state or end an agonizing one.

What's more, our emotional arousal can be amplified by external sources—even something as benign as caffeine. A study from the University of Queensland in Australia tested whether people who had recently ingested caffeine would be more or less open to arguments against voluntary euthanasia, compared to a group who had ingested a placebo. The caffeinated crowd, more subject to feelings of arousal from their drinks, responded more strongly to the arguments and displayed more emotional reactions.

The study proved how easy it is for humans to become emotionally aroused and to increase this arousal. Emotion arrives without our knowledge and amplifies thanks to elements out of our control. We feel that emotions are normal, and acting like a robot is typically discouraged in most aspects of life. That's why emotional arousal can be a dangerous thing—it's both covert and slippery, but also encouraged by statements such as "get in touch with your emotions."

So how exactly does emotional arousal affect us? What's the process from stimulus to reaction, from impulse to full-blown psychological triggers, and how on earth do we dial it back once we're on that path? How can we sit calmly at one moment, then suddenly feel that calling someone a hundred times a day is an acceptable course of action?

Emotional Arousal and Evolution

In general, we feel some kind of emotion twenty-four hours a day. We may even be aware when we're feeling emotions, at least in a physiological sense: our hearts flutter, our stomachs sink, our hands tingle. Humans are emotional beings—it's part of life. But it's criminally easy for that arousal to extend into a second phase that's uncontrollable and risky. That's when extreme emotional arousal sets off our psychological triggers.

These moments are marked by elevated physiological signs and anxiety or excitement. This activity can be extraordinarily potent—and potentially unsafe to ourselves and those around us. Uncontrolled, unconscious and exaggerated emotional reactions can take on a life of their own.

Intense emotions that can be either positive or negative include love, fear, anger, and curiosity. In small doses, these feelings are a normal part of the human experience. But any of those can overpower our self-control and cause us to act in a thoughtless way, like excess energy or pressure that needs to be discharged. (How might even curiosity be negative? How about the impulse of curiosity causing you to embark in extremely risky and dangerous behavior, such as experimenting with illegal drugs?)

We generally receive stimulation through our senses: sight, sound, smell, touch, or taste. When we perceive a stimulus that arouses us, chemicals released by the body flow into the brain. The chemicals animate emotional response via our amygdala while decreasing the function of our prefrontal cortex, which controls our rational, measured, analytical thinking. We then hold less control over conscious responses, and the body experiences physical unrest and prepares itself to go into battle.

The well-known flight-or-fight response is an example of this kind of emotional stimulation. It is a stage in which one experiences *extreme* emotional and physical arousal. Some of us are endowed with arousal responses that are constantly vigilant—seemingly anything can push these folks into red-alert situations in which they scream, run, cry, get angry, or accuse others. Others don't get their buttons pushed as easily and need a stronger stimulus to activate their emotional arousal responses. Depending on which profile a person fits, they process their decision to fight or flee accordingly. The more stimulation we receive, the more aroused we get.

Being in a state of arousal may seem exciting on paper. But it also causes our reason and ability to act logically to go haywire. We make decisions based on what's happening *right now,* strictly in response to the emotions that we're feeling. These emotions make it seem as if they represent reality, rather than just a temporary state of mind. For our purposes, they *are* reality, and we can only operate within the reality we currently feel. In that state of irrationality, we instinctively want to boost positive emotions and cut negative ones in a desperate manner. Our brain is usually removed from this decision altogether.

Survival Instincts

Emotional arousal, when described this way, can seem like a bit of a design flaw in human beings. To the contrary, our emotions are a part of our evolutionary biology and fundamental to our survival instincts. Our instincts, including and most especially our "fight or flight response," evolved over time to keep us safe. This is our in-built biological response to threat or danger in the environment—and our emotions are a part of it. These are powerful forces, and they can absolutely influence us to behave in certain ways.

In a stressful or dangerous situation, the hypothalamus is engaged and stimulated to release chemical messengers—hormones—throughout the body to signal the need to respond to the situation at hand. Adrenaline is a key hormone, and gets our heart racing, blood pumping and senses on hyper-alert.

All of this prepares us to act toward our survival. This process certainly has its uses, but anyone who suffers from an anxiety disorder, as just one example, will know that these mechanisms can also malfunction.

These evolved survival instincts are not just about keeping us away from danger—they're about survival in general, and that also includes our choice of mate. Who we find attractive may be a far more unconscious and physiological process than we give it credit for. The BBC once produced a show in conjunction with Newcastle University, ultimately demonstrating how people *really* choose their partners: based on scent. The idea is that we have evolved the ability to unconsciously detect those partners who are most likely to be a good genetic match for us, with an immune system that is complementary to our own, so that we have the healthiest possible offspring.

The BBC study found that men were most attracted to the *smell of the worn T-shirts* of women who had the most dissimilar immune system types from themselves. They concluded that where survival is concerned, human beings have evolved powerful instincts and impulses that drive their behavior—even if you might think your attraction is because your date is good-looking and intelligent!

What does all this tell us about emotional arousal? Well, emotional arousal and our own inbuilt, evolution-acquired survival instincts may have a lot in common. They can both act as triggers for our behavior, in one way or another. And in many cases, they may appear as one and the same thing. It starts with our sense perceptions (sight, sounds etc.) and our learnt responses to them. There is a neurological component as certain brain regions are engaged, and these correspond to certain emotional states that cause us to respond and act in specific ways.

Most of us in the modern world are unlikely to face routine, immediate threats to our survival—but we nevertheless still possess the same fight-or-flight brain mechanisms. Your body will release adrenaline in response to a *perceived* threat—that could be a dirty look from your boss, a bill in the mail or some vague worry keeping you up late at night. Your body responds *physically*, in the same way it would to a physical threat.

Knowing all this about how we have evolved as human beings and the inherited physiological machinery we are all working with, we can make intelligent and informed decisions for ourselves. There is nothing inherently wrong with emotion, or with the fight or flight response, or with these unconscious, impulsive reactions. But that doesn't mean we need to be at their mercy, either.

The trouble comes in getting carried away with emotion and evolved physiological processes in a way that never gives our higher, rational selves a chance to weigh in—for our own benefit. When we understand that our own biology could be acting as a trigger for certain psychological states and unwanted behavior, we can start to take conscious control.

Be glad that your body works as it does—your fight or flight response will kick in when you need it most, i.e. when there simply *isn't time* to mill over the most rational course of action. Adrenaline is almost a miracle chemical—it helps us feel less pain, gives us a boost of strength and energy, and heightens our senses, allowing us to act at full capacity. But that doesn't mean you can let this unconscious, more "animal" side of your nature run the show 24/7.

Let's return to those potent emotions—love and fear. We now know that part of what makes them so powerful and irresistible is that they are programmed in our very bodies, and have been a part of our makeup since the dawn of our species. If you meet someone one day, you may have a "love at first sight" moment where all at once, you're hit with a flood of strong, positive emotions for this person.

Unaware that what you are experiencing is a heady cocktail of hormones, endorphins and, yes, adrenaline, you go along with your obsession, chemically and neurochemically frothed up into strong emotions we all recognize as infatuation, chemistry, lust, a crush or full-on love. Sure, your immune systems may be highly compatible and there's something about the pheromones this stranger is sending off that makes them seem almost irresistible. This causes you to completely overlook all the information that your more rational self would pay more attention to: you have a twenty-year age gap, they don't properly speak your language, they don't have a job and, oh, you're also married.

Many people can even get addicted to these feelings of infatuation in the way others get hooked on the thrill they get from extreme sports. What's happening is that evolution has designed a physiological mechanism that's somewhat effective, but nowhere near a replacement for self-discipline, rational thought, logic or critical thinking. Unless this person deliberately stops and sees their emotional arousal for what it is, they will never give themselves the chance to let their higher minds step in.

Another example is fear. A man may decide that making necessary changes in his life is simply too frightening, and so he holds off, never reaching his potential, never challenging himself. His body's knee-jerk fear response may well have served his ancestors well, but the same thing that helped them survive in the past may ironically hinder him—that is, until he can understand what is happening and deliberately work with his psychological triggers, rather than simply being at their mercy.

Again, the goal is not to become an emotionless robot—emotions are a normal and valuable part of life. However, being older and more entrenched evolutionarily speaking, emotions leap to the fore while our more recently developed rational mind lags behind. If we ever hope to gain self-mastery, to understand ourselves and to strengthen our will and efficacy in life, we need to learn how to see emotions for what they are, and make sure our rational selves are getting a say in things, too. Because although "survival" may have looked like one thing to our ancient ancestors, for the modern human being, survival also means self-awareness, responsibility and emotional regulation.

The Six Basic Emotions

It's almost impossible to prevent emotions from being a part of our daily lives. It is, however, possible to keep them in a certain level of check. Since emotional responses arrive without much warning, it's beneficial to get familiar with them so we can mitigate the effects they have on us and those around us. Recognizing these feelings when they hit gives us a greater ability to control ourselves and our behaviors. Let's attempt to understand how they manifest and how to short-circuit that process.

In 1976 Paul Ekman, a highly influential psychologist from the University of California at San Francisco, developed a list of six universal emotions (along with the specific facial expressions that display them). One emotion is positive, four are negative, and one can be either:

- **Happiness**

- **Sadness**

- **Anger**

- **Disgust**

- **Fear**

- **Surprise**

Various other studies have yielded different numbers of emotions, ranging from four to seven, but for our purposes, six is sufficient. You may have even been surprised to see surprise and disgust categorized as emotions. Remember that emotions are normal and healthy, but overarousal can lead to regrettable behavior and decisions.

Happiness. A state of emotional peace and fulfillment, happiness is the primary goal for pretty much all of us. Neurochemically, happiness is associated with endorphins, serotonin, dopamine and oxytocin. This is the emotional state that has us feeling open and responsive to the world, hopeful, optimistic and warm. Happiness can trigger us to act generously, to take risks and face our fears, to reach out to others socially, to create, to explore or simply to celebrate.

Once we attain happiness we work to keep it going by recreating it as much as we can. We ride that roller coaster five times in a row, we go to that day spa again, and we return to the same bar where all our friends hang out and laugh.

But there's a breaking point where these positive emotions can produce negative outcomes; when our emotional arousal is so intense, our pursuit of happiness can turn irrational, dangerous, overindulgent, and unhealthy. This is when we turn into hedonists and forsake all else for pleasure and happiness: for instance, drug addiction, developing a dark narcissism about our appearance, having drinking problems.

Sadness. Despair, depression, grief, and loss are, unfortunately, extraordinarily powerful emotions that produce some of the most troublesome states of mind. They can trigger frightening conditions of hopelessness and efforts to emotionally lubricate oneself.

When we're feeling sad, it's as though we shut down and close off to the world. We no longer seek to explore, take chances, ask questions, or express ourselves. We are pessimistic and interpret things negatively, and shy away from others, trapped in the certainty that we know it will all work out badly. Being sad, we may not feel resilient or confident in ourselves; there simply seems to be no point to anything. We may be triggered to numb ourselves down, to escape, to blame others, to retreat into denial or even a secondary emotion, like anger.

The breakup of a relationship, the death of a loved one, the loss of a job or tragic turns in world events can release waves of sadness. When we get too sad, we get triggered to escape or abbreviate the experience as soon as possible, whether through denial, substance abuse, or withdrawal from public life. The worst cases can lead to harming oneself or taking one's own life.

Anger. Anger is a more wrathful, more malicious negative emotion than sadness. Anger can be a product of many of the same events as sadness (breakup, death, job loss, and so forth). But where sadness infers a lessening or loss of our stature or being, anger makes us seek justice or vengeance— for wrongs to be righted or for someone to "pay." We want someone to pay, and we want it right now.

Of all the emotions, perhaps anger is the most likely to trigger real-world action. While anger at a genuine slight can help us to act to reaffirm our boundaries and defend ourselves, some anger is irrational and destructive. Anger can trigger all sorts of narratives and justifications to explain why someone deserves our wrath, and can energize us to start making plans—even if they're not the best thought through or well-intentioned plans!

Anger speaks more directly to offenses to our ego, which prompts a more energetic response: it can trigger desires for revenge, retribution, or destruction. Anger is more easily projected than sadness—an angry person is more likely to find external targets for their efforts. When we're overly angry we're triggered to scream out loud, pound our fists in a wall, or throw a flower vase across the room. We might even create elaborate vengeance schemes. Instead of dwelling in internal misery, an angry person might act out their destructive tendencies on other people or objects.

Disgust. Disgust can be hard to tell apart from anger. Generally speaking, disgust happens when we get offended by something in some way. It doesn't need to be directed at us; it's just a feeling of offense and *disturbance* by something we perceive. We feel disgusted when we smell a carton of spoiled milk or when someone tells a racist joke or when we see someone being pushed into a puddle of mud.

We deal with disgust more indirectly than we deal with anger. We still want to rectify the situation as quickly as possible—we want someone to answer for creating a disgusting and offensive situation, or we want the situation pushed out of sight immediately. If someone's moral failings disgust us, we usually complain to someone else about it, as opposed to the person who's disgusting us. If it's a physical disgust—something that smells or looks bad—we throw it out and clean up as much as we can. Disgust can especially trigger traits and actions associated with obsessive-compulsive disorder (OCD).

Fear. We covered how fear can take control of your brain in the last chapter—when we perceive threats to our being or happiness, we can get triggered into developing full-fledged phobias. When we are too deep in fear, we just want to make it stop. This can make us completely paralyzed or throw us into violent, immediate action to make our anxiety cease. Fear can trigger a range of behaviors—avoiding the situation, getting obsessed with it, blowing things out of proportion, feeling paralyzed or numb, failing to act, becoming confused or even blaming others or looking to them to rescue you.

Surprise. This, of course, is the immediate occurrence of the unexpected, either positive or negative. Really, it can cause any of the other emotions to develop to their fullest extent. Surprise is arguably the most volatile of these emotions because of its suddenness. When we're overly surprised we're triggered to react in shock; afterward, the brain then quickly analyzes the situation to decide whether it's a good shock or a bad one. Shock can make us respond in any number of ways and is the least predictable of emotions.

It happens when someone having a birthday opens the door on a surprise party or when somebody looks at their bank statement and sees a bunch of withdrawals they didn't authorize. Surprise seizes our cognition and drastically reorients our attention. Our triggered reactions can include a dropped jaw, raised eyebrows, or an outburst of expletives. In the more medium term, surprise can morph into another emotion, or trigger us to act in defensive or panicked ways, if the surprise was unpleasant.

As you can see, too much of any emotion, in one way or another, demands quick, strong action to further a pleasurable emotion or subdue a painful one. And as we know by now, quick, strong action does not typically lead to smart decisions.

Control Your GABA

Since attempting to all-out prohibit these universal emotions is futile, our goal is to keep their triggers from spinning out of control. Our goal is to cultivate awareness even in the midst of these fundamentally unconscious processes. The actual physiological prevention method is to help the amygdala and limbic system *slow down* through calming and reducing stress levels. To do that, we have to call up and increase our GABA.

What is GABA? It stands for gamma-aminobutyric acid, and it's the main inhibitive neurotransmitter in our brains; its primary function is to reduce the activity of nerve cells and neurons—in other words, it regulates emotional arousal. Approximately 20 percent of the brain's neurons release GABA, which curtails the action of all the neurons it touches. That reduces the chance the neurons will activate, which means they'll be much less likely to stress us out.

Science has determined that GABA is a major player in treating adverse psychological conditions like anxiety and depression. It has an organic tranquilizing effect on the neurons that fire up those feelings. We can use this fact to our advantage. One of the best ways to increase your GABA and reduce emotional arousal is simple, easy breathing exercises.

This technique has surely been around for thousands of years, but it has been popularized in recent years by Navy SEALs, an elite branch of the United States Navy. For Navy SEALs, succumbing to undesirable responses will mean the difference between life and death. As you might expect, they've developed some techniques that help them maintain clear mental states even in the most dangerous and stressful environments.

One of those techniques that anybody can easily use is what's known as box breathing. When SEALs recognize that they are feeling overwhelmed, they regain control by focusing on their breath—breathing in for four seconds, holding for four seconds, and then out for four seconds, and repeating until you can feel your heart rate slow down and normalize. All it takes is twelve seconds. To begin with, attempt three rounds. If you've made it to the end of three rounds and your heart is still pumping with rage or fear, carry on for three more rounds, and so on.

An aroused mind is an inefficient and harmful mind, and so it is crucial for you to be able to remain calm to make rational decisions. You may not be able to control arousal once it's fully unleashed, but you can moderate it. Box breathing is simple to implement, and if it works for Navy SEALs, it can certainly work for the rest of us. The technique itself is easy, but the real key is to be able to recognize when your arousal might spiral out of control and sabotage your self-discipline.

For this, you can look to your physiology. Whenever you feel your heart beginning to race or your palms starting to sweat, try focusing on your breath to rein in your undesirable reactions. If you can use box breathing at the first hint of physical arousal or stress, you will fare well because you will be able to rein your emotions in before they explode out of control. It's easier to prevent overarousal rather than manage it—and practice definitely makes perfect in this case.

Meditation practices also often involve focusing on the breath and have a similar effect of reducing fight-or-flight instincts. However you go about it, controlling emotional arousal can make a world of difference. Maybe you'll use these tactics the next time you're anxiously anticipating speaking in front of an audience or taking an intense and important exam. Whatever it is that causes you too much of a singular emotion, you'll be more adept to handle it with a clear mental state.

The power of emotions is unquestionable. They're the most pertinent and poignant reasons for us to do anything, and they produce the most active and forceful psychological triggers one can experience. They produce our most beloved romantic comedies as well. But too much of a good thing is indeed still *too much*.

Takeaways:

- Emotions are the cause of some of our weakest and most impulsive moments. This shouldn't be surprising—just consider how insane some of us act when mating and dating. That's because when emotions take over, they become our reality, and we just want to prolong positive emotions or immediately subdue painful ones.

- Paul Ekman defined six main emotions: happiness, sadness, anger, disgust, fear, and surprise. Too much of any of these can easily lead to irrational and harmful behaviors because emotions are all about instant, immediate, powerful actions. Those are not words typically associated with good decisions.

- Emotional arousal is connected with our instincts, which have remained with our species because in evolutionary terms, they helped us stay safe and survive. If we can understand these mechanisms behind, for example, love and fear, we can work *with* them rather than getting carried away with decisions that might not be in our best interests.

- To control our emotional arousal, we must increase the amount of the neurotransmitter GABA that is in our bloodstream. The easiest way to do this is through box breathing, which is simply taking twelve seconds for each complete breath.

Chapter 4. Human Drives, Motivations, and Desires

This chapter discusses the psychological triggers that are simply the result of natural human drives. Natural drives overlap significantly with emotions, and with our evolutionarily derived impulses and instincts.

What are human drives? They are what has kept our species alive, and in this way, we are really no different from animals. Hunger. Sex. Greed. Selfishness. You get the idea. These are the primal motivations that we share with animals—we just dress them up and make them seem a bit nobler, where animals are transparently direct about their desires.

Granted, we do a lot of things other animals can't. We drive cars, tell jokes, argue about politics, and develop vaccines. But we have managed to survive and adapt all these centuries because of the instinctual drives of our species (and, as we've mentioned, our phobias).

We still have those animal drives, but as with many things discussed in this book, they are not always so useful to us in the modern age. You can feel free to consider them as your appendix—the appendix is what is known as a *vestigial organ*, one that the body has evolved past the point of needing. And yet it is still there, occasionally causing problems, erupting, and needing to be removed.

Our innate human drives have mostly outlived their usefulness, yet they still dictate our actions in powerful ways. They're also more *universal* than many other human triggers because all animals have them to a certain extent. For that reason, they're drives that we can predict or foresee a bit more easily than the others. They unite us all in biological ways.

Still, the triggers that arise from our human drives can make us act just as illogically as anything else. Take hunger, for example.

All living creatures have the common biological imperative to eat food. When a human goes hungry for an extended period of time, the nutrients in his or her bloodstream—such as glucose—gradually dwindle. If the brain isn't getting enough glucose it perceives that it's under some kind of threat, which can make one irritable, prone to outbursts, and angry.

Everybody around that human thinks they have an anger management problem, but they probably just need a sandwich. In earlier days, this would prompt us to binge whenever we found food out in the wild. These days, we still have binging impulses, and a lack of food can profoundly affect our moods and cause hasty, irrational decisions to alleviate that drive. It's not an issue of personality, of psychology, culture, values or upbringing. It's pure impulse.

Our human drives ensure we stay alive and thriving. But what are they exactly, and how do they work? Drives by nature are subconscious and instinctual, but if we think about it, we are not truly propelled by a wide variety of motivations. Only a very small set keep us moving forward—and they're largely the same for all different kinds of people. What has historically put us into motion and continues to do so today?

Selfishness and Self-Interest

Like every other species in the world from houseflies to CEOs, our first duty is to look out for Number One—ourselves. Even the most altruistic, least selfish person in the world still has to do what's necessary to keep them existing before they do anything else. This human drive is deeply established in our biology and our evolution as a species. It's the same survival instinct that made prehistoric man attack their neighbors, and much more recent man engage in warfare over territories and resources. If starvation is coming, we'd prefer others to starve instead of ourselves.

As such, we take measures and actions that we believe will help us most and hurt us least. Whatever the situation, we do what's ideal for us. It's not hard to understand the evolutionary principle behind this—we've always had to protect ourselves and have always sought to find the simplest ways to accomplish our goals. Our natural instinct is to raise our chances of living, enduring, and flourishing when we can. This actually makes us very predictable as a species.

This intuition is ruled by the "pleasure principle," another concept psychologist Sigmund Freud came up with, which plainly states that we seek pleasure and avoid pain. Everything we do and are is premised on the pleasure principle (or "pleasure-pain principle"). Everything we believe, cherish, and think springs from it. Every resolution you make, every deed or effort you complete, and whatever lifestyle or addictions you gratify spring from the pleasure principle. There's no part of your mind, soul, or intellect that is untouched by it. The pleasure principle makes us reach for a candy bar when we crave a sweet reward. It makes us study hard for a test or drag ourselves out of bed to the gym. The pain principle, likewise, keeps us away from being around raw sewage, poverty, and unpleasant people.

The person you are today is a product of how you've determined what brings you pleasure or pain throughout your life and how you've behaved as a result. You can boil down every decision you've ever made to one very simple question: "Will this bring me pleasure or pain, and will it be long-term or short-term?" It's why you go to school, choose the job you choose, and wear the clothes you wear. Whether it's a temporary or permanent condition, whether it's a spontaneous act or a long-range plan, even whether it's unconscious or conscious, this very simple question is at the root of everything.

How might our impulse for self-interest be a psychological trigger for us?

Let's take the pleasure part first. Say someone is a gamer. An overly enthusiastic one. Their idea of comfort and joy is spending a long amount of time immersed in a video game. But this person has a job, and unfortunately for them, it's not being a video game tester. Their objective is just to get through work and do the absolute minimum necessary to meet their requirements. When the day's over they head back home and spend the rest of the evening plunged into *Call of Duty*. This also comes at the expense of proper diet and exercise, outside experience, and a social life. They've made this choice to indulge their pleasure center, for better or worse.

Then there's our imperative to avoid pain. Let's say there's somebody who knows they have to start working out to head off the various physical maladies that come from not being in shape. But they don't like the idea of exerting a lot of effort, or *any* effort, into working out because they fear the discomfort that comes along with it: aching bones and muscles, exhaustion, dehydration, the malodorous properties of sweat. These side effects are either painful or unpleasant, and for this person the drive of pain avoidance is stronger than the drive to improve their health.

The pleasure principle is a huge part of the psychological trigger of innate human drives. The prospect of getting something good can motivate one to start taking action to do so. If the prospect of pleasure is incredibly alluring, you'll motivate desperate and intense action—and the same is true with avoiding incredibly intense pain. Just like with emotions, the more intense, the more irrational behavior is induced. The pleasure principle defines our systems of reward and penalty. Every single animal in the known world works from the exact same basis.

A rat will swim through murky or unnavigable (to them) waters if they know there's a slice of cheese at the end of the journey. Dogs "mark their territory" with urine when they feel threatened by a new living situation or an unfamiliar landscape. A salmon's need to procreate urges it to swim against the current of a river to get back to its comfortable spawning ground. A stockbroker's need for material luxury forces them to peddle junk bonds and questionable investments.

It's arguable that our "higher" needs are also just a means to serve our desire for pleasure and avoidance of pain. Even when we are doing something that superficially seems unpleasant, we may be nevertheless deriving a kind of pleasure from it. For example, a parent may not literally enjoy many of the sacrifices they make for their children's sake, but on the whole they derive enormous satisfaction and pleasure from seeing their children happy.

All of us are part of that universal network of biological urges and the drive to satisfy our perceived needs, and we all have our own system of triggers to set us off to satiate them. In that sense, we humans are no different from other animals—even rats, dogs, salmon, and stockbrokers. Also like those animals, the pleasure-pain principle can trigger us into irrational behavior and the loss of free will. This is how someone seeking relief from anxiety or pain can fall into irrational addiction to harmful substances they *know* are bad for them.

The Path of Least Resistance

Another related aspect of human nature is how humans will seek to do the least amount for the greatest benefit possible. This is otherwise known as seeking *the path of least resistance*—the human drive for energy conservation and sloth. There are multiple ways of looking at this human drive. It can be an evolved impulse to conserve energy based on unpredictable dangers and risks, or it can simply be a preference for inertia and laziness.

None of us has infinite time and resources, and so it follows that if there are two courses of action with the same result, but one requires less of an investment of these limited resources, then we would go with that one. Essentially, weighing up the costs and benefits of our actions and the rewards we can expect is a major driver of our behavior.

Suppose you'd like to become a journalist. Your heroes are reporters who do investigative research. They're tireless journalists who delve deeply into their subject matter—they question their subjects rigorously, they plow through years of back paperwork to find relevant incidents, they constantly work on finding new topics or situations to report about, and they log a lot of mileage traveling to and from locations in their stories.

But you either don't have the ability to do that kind of labor-intensive work or you just don't want to. You can still write, though. You can tailor your writing to more opinionated or speculative journalism in which you can get away with lighter research, form a perspective derived from your own beliefs and ideologies, and write colorfully detailed viewpoints for which stringent research rules don't necessarily apply.

There's a need for heavily researched journalism, and there's a need for editorial commentary. Both involve hard work to some extent. But one requires a more free-flowing kind of work that might be more suited to your lifestyle and overall goals.

This example demonstrates the law of the path of least resistance. When we want to achieve something and have multiple ways to do so, humans will always select the course that needs the least effort. Whatever course offers the least discomfort, the least action, and the least investment is the one we'll take.

Maybe you need a birthday cake for a friend's party—you could make one from scratch or buy one from the supermarket. If your friend will be just as pleased either way, it isn't rational to waste time making a cake from scratch. Why not use that saved time to maximize on something else?

Humans perceive effort just as we do materials and planning: as an expense. Computer technicians need circuit boards to work on and knowledge of how to do so—but they also need to turn the screwdrivers themselves, which is why you pay them for costs and labor. We're programmed to seek the easiest way to get stuff done because at heart we all want to be slackers.

The path of least resistance makes people think of laziness, but it's also the principle behind *elegance*, sufficiency and efficient use of resources. It's smart, in other words, and all about using the resources you have in the best way possible to maximize outcomes. When used mindfully and rationally, the path of least resistance can be a great way to seek the "shortest distance between two points."

But the path of least resistance can also be a psychological trigger that causes us to act irrationally. Instead of seeking practical, effective ways to get what we want, we defer to maintaining the status quo that's making us unsatisfied in the first place. That's an irrational state of mind.

A study conducted by University College London boosts the notion that we'd rather take the easy way in a given task. Subjects were shown a moving cloud of dots on a computer screen and were instructed to use a handle in each of their hands to indicate whether the dots were moving to the left or the right. During the trial, researchers made one of the handles more force-resistant and harder to move. When this happened, the subjects were more likely to move the handle that was easier for them to operate—even if it corresponded to the wrong answer (if the dots were moving left but their left handle was harder to move, they'd opt for the right).

Dr. Nobuhiro Hagura, who administered the test, concluded that "The gradual change in the effort of responding caused a change in how the brain interpreted the visual input. Importantly, this change happened automatically, without any awareness or deliberate strategy... The motor response that we use to report our decisions can actually influence the decision about what we have seen."

So even if our brains perceive a certain task through visual or sensory cues, they will always seek to find bypasses around efforts that could be less comfortable or more inconvenient. Whether it takes more time, costs more money, inflicts more pain, or even makes an action the least bit bothersome, the brain is always looking for shortcuts.

That, in turn, produces a psychological trigger that affects our actions. Let's say someone has the rather generalized goal of being "comfortable." They want a living situation where they're content, safe, and happy. Perhaps they think being happy ultimately involves owning a house, being financially secure, having a family, or being free to pursue a lot of different interests. There are many ways to obtain this kind of situation, but it's safe to say the large majority of them, at some point, require a lot of work.

But maybe this person doesn't want to work that hard—it will cause effort, pain, or some other kind of unpleasant situation. So they'll start bargaining with themselves as to how good they can get it if they take the path of least resistance. They don't have to own a house; they just need a roof over their head. They don't need to be rich; they just need to get along somehow. They don't need a family; they have sufficient friends or they're just fine being alone. And they don't need the free time and resources to explore different experiences or try new things; they've got Netflix.

In that case, the path of least resistance is leading to a kind of irrational thought—in the sense that the person doesn't want to engage in much *rational* thought. They can rationally plan how to make their own life better and more comfortable, but they decide it's not worth the work and they'll accept their current situation as a consolation prize. They prioritize ease or a status quo over something beneficial or simply *better*.

So even though they have the power to change their circumstances (and they know that many other people do not have that power), they won't try harder than they have to. This mechanism can keep people trapped even in quite bad situations because changing is perceived to be too difficult. Whether consciously or not, sometimes we make the choice to do nothing and stay lazy, rather than take a path with, well, some resistance.

It's important to note that the path of least resistance isn't always a *bad* thing. Sometimes it's the more effective choice to reduce clutter and obstacles brought on by doing too many things at once. Furthermore, the path of least resistance isn't always one that requires *less* work. Often it requires legitimately hard work, but it might be a kind of labor you're more used to doing and can perform more easily than others can. The important thing is to know yourself, your abilities, and what you can handle—and to follow those cues to find the best path to make your goals achievable.

Overall, the path of least resistance is extremely dependable and reliable as far as psychological triggers go. It uses the human drive to seek ease and comfort—or complacency and laziness—to spring our minds into irrational decisions that preserve the current status of things. We think we're just taking things easy, but we're actually letting go of our free will, seduced into energy conservation for no particular purpose.

The Four Human Drives

The two human drives described above are things we can immediately identify and relate to. The next four are more subconscious. Psychologists Paul R.

Lawrence and Nitin Nohria boiled down the whole of human motivation to four basic "drives," each of which comes complete with a bunch of potential psychological triggers.

Once again, these human drives have been employed throughout our evolution to ensure our survival but can also trigger irrational behavior if they go too far. These motivations were mnemonically ordered as "ABCD" so they're easier to remember.

Acquire. What must we obtain or increase our possession of to ensure our survival? The drive to acquire covers everything from material needs (shelter, food, clothes, and so forth) to personal experience (travel, sex, adventure, etc.). It can also include elevated personal status or influence.

The tricky thing about the drive to acquire is that we're not inclined to stop once we have what we want; we simply want more and more. In excess, this sets off our psychological triggers to get what we want beyond what's necessary for our survival.

For example, let's take *Willy Wonka & the Chocolate Factory.* In the book and movie, Wonka decides to open up a tour of his legendary factory to anyone who finds one of five "golden tickets" that he's hidden in five random candy bars. This creates a global mania in which everyone on Earth buys a Wonka candy bar in hopes of acquiring one of the tickets.

The odds are stacked against everyone who partakes since there are only five tickets and millions of candy bars, but the drive to acquire something beyond the mere candy sets everyone off in a buying frenzy (and causes at least one person to make a fake golden ticket). These actions are the products of irrational behavior, triggered by an oversized desire to acquire.

We can also see this impulse in overdrive with people who are avid collectors, or anyone we'd commonly call greedy. This is the kind of person who will buy a new gadget when they have two of the same gadgets at home already, unused. In other words, the unchecked and unconscious need to acquire things is irrational—

obtaining more and more material objects doesn't increase their utility or your comfort. In fact, if you're a hoarder or someone who's gone into debt because of your shopping habit, your drive to acquire is actively harming you and possibly others.

Bond. Historically, humans formed alliances and connections with one another for purposes of having a family and also to better withstand societal or environmental threats. Developing these kinds of social connections and relationships is an inborn need: we're driven to commit to others and experience fulfillment when we've acquired a mutually expressed connection with someone else.

The desire for this kind of bond defines all our social and interpersonal interactions and sets off all the triggers that make us seek companionship. A person going to a bar to make new acquaintances, someone joining a dating service to find long-term (or short-term) romance, and someone joining a historical event society to take part in Civil War reenactments are all examples of how we seek to fill the need for bonds. When we seek to bond, we want to keep loneliness at bay, and you can imagine how that can lead to desperate and impulsive behavior.

The person going to the bar could develop a drinking problem. The person joining a dating service could turn to stalking after being spurned or rejected. The Civil War reenactor could lose all touch with the modern world. At some point their desires to bond were corrupted and reduced to psychological triggers that took away their free will.

To look at this another way, the person who is compulsively driven by this bonding impulse will find themselves needy or constantly craving approval or attention; they'll become the kind of person who leaps into another relationship the second their previous one ends. Being too far enmeshed with others, we lose our independence and power to choose for ourselves—i.e., we are at risk for losing sight of our free will and agency when our identities dissolve into interpersonal relationships.

Those who take bonding too far include women who have no other identity except "mother," young boys who do ridiculous things simply for the honor of belonging to their gang (even if that "gang" is a church group or golf club), or people who act in irrational ways because of infatuated love or ill-conceived patriotism. Our need to belong and feel loved, or even just liked or admired, can be, sadly, a powerful motivator for irrational behavior.

Comprehend. Humans need to be in the know. They seek answers and explanations for the events going on around them and have a natural state of curiosity that drives an impulse to learn, understand, believe, and appreciate their world. The world is a big, scary place, and our intellect and knowledge can help us control and predict the sometimes baffling phenomena we find ourselves surrounded with.

As such, this unique and inherently self-reflective trait in humans has given them a huge advantage over other species in survival across generations—but it's not a drive without its disadvantages.

This drive triggers us into finding education or refined awareness of certain topics. It makes us go to college, attend a training school, or take an online course. It also encourages us to look up information on the web, attend museums and zoos, or watch cooking shows. Anything that provides illumination where there once wasn't is fueled by our need to understand as much as we can.

But it can also lead to irrational behavior, especially if our drive to know leads to an unhealthy or fanatical obsession with a certain thing, topic, or person. In another sense, the endless desire to understand can mask an inability to tolerate uncertainty, to be spontaneous, to relinquish control or accept mistakes or ignorance. Sometimes, ironically, it can be our stubborn desire to feel as though we already know that most prevents us from learning!

Defend. Possibly the first of these four drives to manifest in humans is the need to protect and fight for ourselves, our loved ones, our belief systems, our assets, and our general way of life. Whenever an outside threat is detected (whether it's real or not), humans' sense of alarm activates and triggers the emotional responses of fear or anger.

Of course, the readiest examples of defending ourselves and our loved ones are on the confrontational plane: defending ourselves against physical attacks, challenging bullies, and protecting our families and friends from those with ill intent. But this instinct also makes us do more mundane things: buying insurance, building fences around our yards, reinforcing our home security systems, and getting lawyers.

When it gets to an irrational state, we run the risk of being paranoid: imagining or blowing up threats to our happiness that aren't really there. We think people are engaged in plots to cheat us or we cut ourselves off from the outside world and threaten them if they come too close. Boundaries are good, but if they're too inflexible, they become cages that wall us in and shut us off from life.

These four human drives further emphasize just how we can be pushed or pulled to act in ways that are irrational or impulsive. As with other aspects already considered, it's not the drive, need or instinct itself that is "wrong"—rather, it's a question of the damage we can do when we allow ourselves to get carried away with these tendencies without moderating them with restraint, balance, and rational self-discipline.

The Seven Deadly Sins

The seven deadly sins, probably the most well-known catalog of vices in human history, were devised in the fourth century by a Greek monk. All these sins (or flaws, if you prefer) represent extensions of human desire at the expense of reason or moderation. If the various threads of human nature fall on a continuum, the sins are at the far extreme and need to be guarded against.

They serve as psychological triggers because they express things we really *want* to have but, for whatever reason, can't or don't. But deep down, if we come across the temptation to indulge in any of these sins, we'll be hard-pressed to resist irrational thought.

The seven deadly sins/flaws didn't just come out of the blue. They're categorized the way they are because humans are predisposed to them—they form a big part of our human drives. The more we want to satisfy them, the harder we'll work to get them, and the crazier we'll act. After all, aren't sins the epitome of psychological triggers?

To let oneself get carried away with one or more of these qualities is the ultimate indulgence—the "pleasure" part of the pleasure principle running amok. And it's easy to see how they can turn us into monsters. So what's on the menu?

Pride. In this context, pride is not mere confidence or satisfaction in one's achievements, both of which are perfectly acceptable. Rather, the downside of pride is when one's self-belief lapses into arrogance, in which they consider themselves invincible or better than anyone else. It's pure self-glorification combined with a massive fear of being publicly scorned or embarrassed.

Pride triggers our defense mechanism against blows to our (perceived) reputation or standing. It's the lifeblood of social media wars in which we comprehend differences of opinion as personal affronts. Pride can trigger us into irrational thoughts and acts, like not backing down when we know we're wrong. A side effect of pride is not acknowledging the privilege or luck you've received, and failing to appreciate or show gratitude for other people's contribution to your good fortune.

Greed. The craven desire for money and valuable goods and the presumption that wealth reflects one's personal power is greed. The greedy person wants to accumulate as much capital and objects as they can, to the near-total exclusion of personal relationships, moral codes, or concern for those less fortunate. Greed is irrational because it fails to see any other value in life beside materialistic value— mere *things*.

Greed triggers us to increase our wealth and material belongings and activates an aggressive approach in us to do so. It encourages us to go on online buying sprees or engage in shady business practices. Often it engenders a sense of competition, in which one combatively goes after rivals and enemies to get their prize—like stockbrokers, political candidates, or network executives. At the further end of irrational behavior, greed makes us want to take destructive measures to get what we want—to cheat a business partner, steal a car, or lie to someone to get what we desire.

Envy. The sin of envy is similar to greed—but this time it's personal. Envy is when we go past mere admiration of someone for who they are, what they do, or what they have, and enter the realm of resentment of others' good fortune. Left unchecked, admiration of others can slip into a negative zone, in which we get angry or sad at people who've got what we want.

Envy is triggered by failure or seeing someone get or be something that we want, but believe we can't have. A prime example is the Tonya Harding/Nancy Kerrigan figure-skating story, recently brought back to attention thanks to the acclaimed movie *I, Tonya*.

Harding was envious of Kerrigan's success and (equally as important) her reputation as America's figure-skating sweetheart. It drove Harding to hire a couple of men to attack Kerrigan by whacking her in the knees. Instead of using her mental vision of success as motivation to work harder and stronger, envy gave her the inspiration to commit a physical act of cruelty that just about everyone in America knew she was behind. That's irrational.

Any time we are driven by envy, we are mistakenly assuming that someone else's success and well-being is a threat to our own. It's a state of mind that presumes that success and happiness are limited. Ironically, envy can make us less likely to be the people we want to be because unconsciously, we decide we hate those who could actually serve as our mentors and inspiration.

Wrath. Some folks use "anger" in this spot, but I think "wrath" is the proper term because anger is not always destructive. Wrath is more than just being mad. It's when one goes way past "proper" anger and wants to cause destruction or pain to others.

As we saw previously, anger and fear have their evolutionary advantages—being indignant and angry can help us take necessary action, solidify violated boundaries and summon the energy to make big, scary changes. But wrath continues long after this purpose has been served. Wrath is vindictiveness, the renegade desire to settle scores and cause some collateral damage as well.

Unfortunately, there are way too many real-news items in our world that show the devastating effects of wrath. It triggers people to attack the bodies and identities of other people. Whether it's a bigot berating a person of a different ethnicity in a coffee shop or a terrorist causing wide-scale death and ruin to entire communities, wrath is an insidious element that causes some of the most destructive irrational acts anyone can perform. It can also simply involve wasting hours of time planning out an intricate, but useless, plan of vengeance.

Lust. This is the longing for physical pleasure and bodily desire—all right, let's just come out and say it: sex. This one's tricky because lust plays a part in healthy romantic relationships. But like all the other "sins," when it becomes the dominating driver of one's actions beyond all moderation, it can be troublesome.

Visual stimulation is a primal, very dependable trigger for lust, which explains why pornography is a billion-dollar business. Tactile stimulation, and to a lesser degree stimulation of any of the remaining four senses, also serve as reliable triggers.

But it's vital to not let those urges resolve themselves in irrational, nonconsensual acts. Though our species craves refined sugar, it's bad for us—we need a varied, nutritious and wholesome diet. In the same way, pure animal lust is certainly appealing, but to obtain complete emotional and spiritual health humans require love, respect, honesty, trust and all those other things not necessarily in the front of our minds when lust is running wild.

Lust is one of the more powerful triggers, and the irrational behaviors it can produce are similar to the destructive ones wrath generates: stalking, assault, and violence, not to mention porn addiction, harassment and affairs.

Gluttony. Greed makes us want to possess things, and lust makes us want to feel or sense things. Gluttony, by comparison, makes us want to consume things. The most common association with gluttony, of course, is food and drink—eating and drinking far more than one needs to survive in chase of an unattainable pleasure. A glutton, ironically, doesn't ever really feel full or satisfied—they just keep going and going.

Gluttony applies to anything that we take in without making much effort to produce something back. Sigmund Freud decided that gluttony could partially dislodge unfulfilled feelings of lust, as well. There is something very infantile about gluttony, and getting stuck in endless "feeding" and taking in, rather than getting out into the world to create or give back.

The simple pleasures of encountering food via smell or visual stimulation set off several triggers. They're even more acute when we encounter "comfort food"—dishes that are nutritionally unsound in excess but nonetheless serve to soothe or medicate people in some way. The end result of gluttony is usually overeating, of course, but it can also produce any number of eating disorders, including bulimia.

Sloth. Simply put, sloth is laziness. It's the avoidance of work and responsibility and the desire to just sit around and do nothing—an overextension of the path of least resistance we mentioned earlier. But sloth isn't just about being a slacker, as it applies to more than just physical relaxation. Sloth is not just rest or ease—it's being stagnant and apathetic, seemingly not considering life in general worth the effort.

One can also be slothful in thinking or mentality, especially when confronted with something that might challenge their beliefs. Someone who projects indifference or an uncaring countenance could be said to curate sloth—even if they work harder than anyone else.

It's hard to say what triggers sloth—the idea of something "triggering" inaction could appear a contradictory thought. A depleted self-image or sense of belonging might be one such trigger, as would depression and hopelessness. These triggers can result in anything from eight-hour sofa TV binges to sleeping in or playing hooky from work or school.

Overall, the seven sins represent things we enjoy or at least desire some of the time. As such, they define human drives that motivate us highly and can cause us to act in irrational ways to attain them. And while it's important not to get too self-critical when we feel quick rushes of pride, lust, wrath, or any of the other sins, it's just as vital for us to watch out for the powerful triggers they can set off.

Some consider it counterproductive to try and combat our natural or biological drives; after all, they've supposedly been programmed by forces entirely outside our control. But that's a trap of the mind. While we'll always be defined by our biology, we can watch out for and identify psychological triggers when they're happening to take away excuse and inspire improvement.

Maslow's Hierarchy of Needs

If you read the previous section, you might have wondered—what constitutes lust and what is simply a normal and healthy sexual appetite? Human beings are animals, and all sexually reproducing animals have a drive that compels them to seek sex, don't they? In the same way, food is not exactly something you can go teetotal on—we all need food to survive. Many would argue that we also need social interaction, love, approval, a sense of belonging, purposeful work, and so on.

The seven deadly sins is admittedly a very old-fashioned (not to mention religious) concept. A more modern and humane picture of human behavior takes into account the *reasons* people do what they do—and it's more than just a question of upright or poor character. We can see human drives and motivators as essentially negative, i.e. as destructive impulses that constantly threaten to lead us astray unless we whip them into shape. The deadly sins is the perfect example—stemming in large part from the Christian idea that human beings are essentially wicked by nature.

However, we can also see human drives and motivations in a more neutral or even positive light. In other words, it is not irrationality or evil that drives us, but simply the natural and obvious compulsion to fulfill our needs. According to this viewpoint, we act in the ways we do because it satisfies our human needs, whether those needs are for food, social connection, status, or meaningful work.

Maslow's hierarchy of needs is one of the most famous models in the history of psychology. It employs a pyramid to show how certain human "needs"—like food, sleep, and warmth—are necessary to resolve before more aspirational needs like love, accomplishment, and vocation can be pursued. Maslow's pyramid provides a visual example of how motivation changes and increases after we get what we need at each stage in our lives, which typically coincides with where we are on the hierarchy itself.

When psychology professor Abraham Maslow came along in the 1940s, his theory boiled everything down to one revolutionary idea: human beings are a product of a set of basic human needs, the deprivation of which is the primary cause of most psychological problems. Fulfilling these needs is what drives us on a daily basis.

The hierarchy, now named for him, maps out basic human needs and desires and how they evolve throughout life. It functions like a ladder—if you aren't able to satisfy your more basic, foundational human needs and desires, it is extremely difficult to move forward without stress and dissatisfaction in life. This means your motivations change depending on where you are in the hierarchy.

To illustrate, let's take a look at how our needs and associated motivations change from infancy to adulthood. As infants, we don't feel any need for a career or life satisfaction. We simply need to rest, be fed, and have shelter over our heads. Feeding and survival are our only real needs and desires (as parents of newborns will tell you).

As we grow from infants into children and teenagers, simply staying alive and healthy doesn't bring satisfaction. We hunger for interpersonal relationships and friendships. What drives us is to find a feeling of belonging and community. Then, as we mature into young adults, simply having a great group of friends is no longer enough to satisfy us. It feels empty, actually, without an overall sense of purpose.

If, as adults, we are fortunate enough to be able to provide financial security and stability for ourselves and our families, then our desires and needs can turn outward rather than inward. It's the same reason that people like Warren Buffett and Bill Gates participate in philanthropy to make as big an impact as they can on the world.

The stages of Maslow's hierarchy of needs determine exactly what you're motivated by depending on where you are in the hierarchy.

The first stage is physiological fulfillment. This is easily seen in the daily life of an infant. All that matters to them is that their basic needs for survival are met (i.e., food, water, and shelter). Without security in these aspects, it is difficult for anyone to focus on satisfaction in any other area—in fact, it would actually be harmful to them to seek other forms of satisfaction. So this is the baseline level of fulfillment that must first be met.

The second stage is safety. If someone's belly is full, they have clothes on their back, and they have a roof over their head, they need to find a way to ensure that those things keep on coming. They need to have a secure source of income or resources to increase the certainty and longevity of their safety.

These first two stages are designed to ensure overall survival. Unfortunately, many people never make it out of these first two stages due to unfortunate circumstances, and you can plainly see why they aren't concerned with fulfilling their potential.

The third stage is love and belonging. Now that your survival is ensured, you'll find that it is relatively empty without sharing it with people you care about. Humans are social creatures, and case studies have shown that living in isolation will literally cause insanity and mental instability, no matter how well fed or secure you are. This stage includes relationships with your friends and family and socializing enough so you don't feel that you are failing in your social life.

Of course, this stage is a major sticking point for many people—they are unable to be fulfilled or focus on higher desires because they lack the relationships that create a healthy lifestyle. Isn't it easy to imagine someone who is stuck at a low level of happiness because they don't have any friends?

The fourth stage is self-esteem. You can have relationships, but are they healthy ones that make you feel confident and supported?

This stage is all about how your interactions with others impact your relationship with yourself. This is a very interesting level of maturity in terms of needs because it boils down to self-acceptance. You know you have a healthy level of self-esteem when you can accept yourself even if you are misunderstood or outright disliked by others. For you to get to this stage and have a healthy level of self-esteem, you have to have accumulated certain achievements or earned the respect of others. There is a strong interplay between how you get along with and help others and how you feel about yourself.

The final stage is self-actualization. The highest level of Maslow's hierarchy is self-actualization. This is when you are able to live for something higher than yourself and your needs. You feel that you need to connect with principles that require you to step beyond what is convenient and what is comfortable. This is the plane of morality, creativity, spontaneity, lack of prejudice, and acceptance of reality.

Self-actualization is placed at the top of the pyramid because this is the highest (and last) need people have. All the lower levels have to be met first, before a person can reach this final level. You know you are working with somebody who operates at a truly high level when they do not focus so much on what is important to them personally, their self-esteem, or how other people perceive them. This is the stage people are at when they say they want to find their calling and purpose in life.

Maslow's theory may not accurately describe all of our daily desires, but it does provide an inventory for the broad strokes of what we want in life. Though many might disagree with the exact needs he lists, or indeed their relative order, the theory is still useful in that it reminds us that certain needs will always need to be fulfilled before others can be considered.

It's also a useful way to think about human drives in a positive and aspirational manner. Maslow believed that psychologists spent too much time studying malfunction, when they should be looking at what makes a healthy, happy human being. Thus, his theory doesn't really address those truly unhealthy, irrational or harmful human behaviors, i.e. the negative motivators.

As useful as the theory is, you can probably agree that not all of us are always motivated by the innocent and natural drive to satisfy our needs. If you are reading this book, you're likely interested in precisely those harmful psychological mechanisms that clearly *don't* serve any good end. This is the topic of our next section.

Protecting Pride Above All Else

The final drive that clouds our judgment and creates a perception far removed from reality is our natural sense of self-defense. Here, self-defense is about how we are able to maintain a healthy sense of self-esteem by strategically plugging our ears, digging our heels in, and tuning others out. Our need to preserve self-esteem can drive us to ridiculous heights.

We don't want to feel bad about ourselves, and we will spin reality to keep our self-perception positive. It's the art of intentional ignorance and denial—because sometimes, that's just what we need to function and get by. If we feel too low about ourselves on a constant basis, we'll begin to knock on the door of depression and all that entails. Much like the D portion of the ABCD model of human drives, this makes us desperate to feel good about ourselves.

For instance, let's suppose you are the lowest performer at your job. Everyone at the office seems to know it. Such a situation is a hard blow to our pride, and our egos might not accept the objective reality of being the worst performer in the building who only got there because of a family connection. So what happens? We start to rationalize, justify, or utilize some type of defense mechanism to make ourselves feel better.

The objective truth be damned, you will engage in caveats, exceptions, explanations, and justifications for why your performance is low yet can be excused.

You'll catch yourself saying things like, "Well, at least I'm the most fit person in the office;" or "Well, I don't let my job define me; I have a life outside of this to focus on;" or even "I'm actually really in the top three; the data just doesn't show it." These are statements designed to preserve your dignity and self-esteem in any way possible. That's what self-defense of your psyche is.

Even though you might understand the negative reality you are facing, you find different angles to look at it in order to maintain an overall healthy outlook on life.

The first rebuttal the person used in the situation above was about finding something else of value to rank themselves on, and the second rebuttal was about giving a reason *why* their job performance was acceptably lower. The third statement was simply denial. None of these justifications actually helped the situation— but they did help the person who was speaking them, affording them a small way to deflect a painful reality and maintain their sanity.

Generally, these are known as defense mechanisms or rationalizations—and they are almost always irrational ways of viewing reality.

Defense mechanisms are the methods we use consciously or subconsciously to deflect tension or negativity from our ego, pride, and self-esteem. These methods keep us whole when times are tough.

The origin of the term comes from Sigmund Freud (again), who posited that defense mechanisms were necessary to protect the ego. Three of the most widespread defense mechanisms are denial, intellectualization, and rationalization.

Denial is one of the most classic defense mechanisms because it is easy to use. "No, I don't believe that report ranking all of the employees. There's no way I can be last. Not in this world."

What is true is simply claimed to be false, as if that makes everything go away. We are acting as if a negative fact doesn't exist, and thus, there is nothing to be dragged down about. Sometimes we don't realize when we do this, especially in situations that are so dire they actually appear fantastical to us. All you have to do is say *no* often enough and you might begin to believe yourself, and that's where the appeal of denial lies. You are actually changing your reality, where other defense mechanisms merely spin the truth to be acceptable. Denial is actually the most irrational defense mechanism, because even if there is a dire problem, it is ignored and never fixed. If someone continued to persist in the belief they were an excellent driver, despite a string of accidents in the past year, it's unlikely they would ever seek to practice their driving skills.

Intellectualization is when you deal with negativity or threats to your self-esteem by pushing emotion aside and using logic to make yourself feel better.

This is an attempt to tell yourself that things are not as bad as they seem. For example, you start to console yourself about how the job market is healthy and you've gained valuable skills by learning how low you rank in the office. The negative event has occurred, but you aren't focusing on it or the consequences—you are focusing on the logical way forward and painting the best-case scenario for yourself. This technique isn't necessarily wrong, but it's diverting focus away from reality and only paying attention to an angle that makes you feel good about yourself.

Rationalization is when you explain away something negative.

It is the art of making excuses. The bad behavior or fact still remains, but it is turned into something unavoidable because of circumstances out of your control. The bottom line is that anything negative is not your fault and you shouldn't be held accountable for it. It's never a besmirching of your abilities. Rationalization is extremely convenient, and you are only limited by your imagination.

For instance, if you want to talk to an attractive stranger but keep chickening out, this is something that could be construed as negative. However, a very common rationalization of this lack of action would be to simply say they weren't really that cute, they appeared preoccupied or mean, or you were too tired at that point in the night.

These might appear to be flimsy excuses, but they are the small escape paths your psyche needs in order to feel good about itself. It's easier to portray someone as ugly or mean than to come to grips with the fact that you were deathly afraid of rejection or that you were nauseous all night thinking about it, only to fail. The latter leads to shame and embarrassment, while the former leads to "Well, there's always next time!"

Rationalization is the embodiment of the *sour grapes fable*. A fox wanted to reach some grapes at the top of a bush, but he couldn't leap high enough. To make himself feel better about his lack of leaping ability and to comfort himself about his lack of grapes, he told himself the grapes looked sour, anyway, so he wasn't missing out. He was still hungry, but he'd rather be hungry than hurt his pride.

Rationalization can also help us feel at peace with poor decisions we've made with phrases such as "It was going to happen at some point, anyway" or "The price won't go much lower, anyway." You'll hear these when you are grappling with buyer's remorse or buying something at a high price when it was discounted the following day.

Rationalization ensures you never have to face failure, rejection, or negativity. It's always someone else's fault!

So while comforting, these defense mechanisms skew reality and lead to overall self-defeating behaviors. People will make more and more bad decisions, resist growth, ignore opportunity, and generally act against their own interests—only acting in support of their ego. A life dictated by self-protection does not bode well in the long run.

Takeaways:

- Human drives are perhaps the epitome of psychological triggers. They have kept our species alive, but those instincts don't transfer so well to the modern age.

Thankfully, these human drives are relatively predictable because of how universal they are—within all people, and animals as well!

- The first human drive is selfishness and self-interest. We want to benefit from our behavior, and we want to benefit over other people. Not too surprising. Taken to the extreme, this drives us to antisocial and alienating behaviors.

- Another human drive is the preference for the path of least resistance. We seek the most benefit for the least amount of work on a consistent basis. Whether it's energy conservation or sloth, this is something that makes us act irrationally.

- ABCD—this is another model for human drives. It stands for acquire, bond, comprehend, and defend. Again, taken to the extreme, these can trigger all sorts of frightful behavior.

- Similarly, the classic seven sins represent things we want but shouldn't indulge in. You could probably classify them as psychological triggers themselves, which cause people to act irrationally.

- Maslow's famous theory shows us that human behavior is an attempt to satisfy various human needs, which fall on a hierarchy, with the most basic physiological and safety requirements needing to be fulfilled before we can consider the higher needs. The pinnacle is self-actualization, which is the point at which a human being fulfills their entire potential.
- The final natural human drive is self-defense—more specifically, defense of the ego and sense of pride. This is done through defense mechanisms, which actually skew your sense of reality. The most widespread ones are denial, rationalization, and intellectualization.

Chapter 5. Hunches and Gut Reactions

In this chapter, we'll discuss how our minds rely on our gut reactions and hunches and how they guide our decisions—whether they're good choices or bad ones. It's a somewhat troublesome topic, because many, if not most, of our initial reactions or instincts about situations lead to snap judgments and premature findings. These lead to bad results 99 times out of 100, and that one time it didn't probably isn't that good, either.

By definition, instincts and gut reactions spring from a lack of data. They're emotional responses made with little or no information at all. What is a hunch, really? It's just a feeling that something is true or not based on anything tangible.

People depend on hunches because they're easy and we err on the side of laziness, which means they can trigger irrational reactions and behaviors that make the situations worse. How many times have we applied stereotypes or biases to judge a certain person or situation, just because we didn't think we had time to make more careful considerations? Probably a lot more than we'd like to admit.

At other times, our instincts activate when we're tricked into believing something by outside forces. For instance, the advertising profession lives off this kind of seduction. We're fed images and ideals about how great our lives can be if we buy a certain product or take up a certain kind of program. That kind of persuasion feeds into our instincts, creating emotional arousal and leading us to irrational acts: spending money we don't have or taking risks we're not prepared for.

As a result of this pressure, you buy the car. Four weeks later it breaks down in traffic and you know you were at least partially hoodwinked. Your instincts turned out to be wrong, manipulated by a slick salesman. You should have sought out more information or at least slept on it.

This chapter discusses how our minds are programmed to work and how our default settings don't always work in our favor. We want to make snap judgments and jump to conclusions whenever we can because it's convenient (and again, helpful for our continued survival as a species). Sometimes, we even think that the world should be simple enough that our gut instincts should guide us successfully through whatever we want to engage in. But by doing so, we leave out a lot of important information we need to consider before acting. This also leads to flat-out wrong ways of thinking: stereotypes, incorrect assumptions, and falsehoods.

Sometimes we call our quick decisions "instinct" or "intuition," but far too often they just serve as excuses for our not wanting to gain all the facts we need or form good judgments. First, we'll start with the psychological bases for what drives us to make split-second decisions under the guise of being well-informed: schemas and heuristics.

Schemas and Heuristics

How we learn and experience the world throughout our lives constantly informs our decisions, judgments, and actions. Our methods and systems for dealing with the world come from our exposure to certain situations. Of course, the types of experiences we've already had pale in comparison to the number of situations we've yet to run into in the real world.

But we can only use what we know, and thus, we project our old experiences onto new situations we find ourselves in. For all intents and purposes, this is our version of reality, even though you might be thinking that this makes reality incredibly subjective, contextual, and subject to different interpretations. It does.

For better or worse, these limited experiences are what form our gut instincts, and clearly they are not all correct. In essence, we are creating a model of the world and then using that model to help us make assessments and predictions about the world—but the thing about a model is that it is always necessarily simplified. The "territory is not the map," as they say, and errors are inevitable. Thus, when you combine subjective experience with haste, we are pulled into irrational acts.

There are generally two ways in which we organize the limited information we have about the world: schemas and heuristics. They serve to put what we know about the world into action and facilitate quick decision-making. Each of them goes a long way in producing our psychological triggers.

Schemas. A schema is a model by which we arrange and decipher the information we're currently receiving. It allows us to say, "Okay, based on these three factors I can observe, I know what this is and how to act." Imagine a schema as a snapshot of a certain situation, and using that snapshot to arrange unfamiliar information.

Introduced by psychologist Jean Piaget, schemas are contextual, and we have schemas for all different types of situations. Schemas develop throughout our entire lives, though they're at their most prevalent when we're learning about something for the first time. But while schemas are extremely useful, they can steer us toward unwarranted biases or errors.

For example, a young child comes across a little red wagon. She asks her parents what it is, and they tell her it's a wagon. It moves around on four wheels and has a compartment in which you place things. Based on her experience and knowledge, the child now has a schema for identifying a "wagon."

Sometime later, this child sees a sports car. She remarks to her parents, "Look, a wagon!" She says this because the sports car has four wheels and moves around, and to her that means it's a wagon. Her parents then have to explain to her that it's not—it's a sports car. It's much bigger than the wagon. It's also driven by a steering wheel instead of being pulled along by a handle. It has doors and a roof, which the wagon doesn't have.

This simplistic anecdote shows how a schema develops—a model for identifying wagons and what wheels represent. "Okay," the child might say, "so based on these factors, I know what a wagon is and what a car is."

When the child first saw the wagon and her parents explained it to her, she immediately had a frame of reference: a wagon has four wheels and moves. When she saw the sports car, she used that framework to decide it was a wagon, until her parents corrected her. Her schema, therefore, becomes more refined and exact. Next time, the child might see a go-cart and decide it's a wagon, and she might see a minivan and decide it's a sports car. She'll be corrected again, and her schema will be further redefined. "Okay, so based on these factors, I know what a wagon is, what a car is, what a minivan is, and what a motorcycle is."

As you can see, schemas can be created on a disturbingly small amount of information, and yet we can take those beliefs far into our lives if they are not corrected. Much of the time, even if they are corrected and refined, they are still incomplete. Developing contextual schemas—ranging from identifying vehicles to learning how to act during a visit to the doctor's office to choosing different types of furniture—is key to making quick decisions.

We have schemas for literally everything we encounter, and when we're experiencing the world, those schemas go through multiple transformations. But as we grow older, our schemas become more settled. We reach conclusions about things because we figure our schemas have enough information—but frequently, we don't have it, or we don't listen to it. The snapshot that we use to navigate unfamiliar situations might be skewed and flawed, but we can't tell the difference.

At that point, our schemas become vessels through which we only see "truths" that confirm the opinions and interpretations we already have. We never really consider or remember that our schemas are schemas—we mistakenly assume we are dealing with reality itself, and not a picture of reality. Where schemas may occasionally have aided gut instincts, they can easily lead us astray.

This is called "confirmation bias," and it's a major source of stereotypes, prejudices, and faulty assumptions. Absorbing new information that doesn't conform to our presumed beliefs is difficult at best and impossible at worst. Without that information, our cognitive bias can lead to unsound judgments and irrational behaviors—our schemas become cemented over time and we make worse and worse decisions. "Okay, so based on these factors (three of which are incorrectly interpreted...)"

It should be easy to see how this can result in irrational behavior: our schemas exclude us from absorbing rational information because it doesn't fit into our worldview, and thus, we create an alternative reality. Suppose the young child from earlier never had the difference between wagons and cars explained to her or that it had been explained incorrectly or in a confusing way. Now her conception of things with four wheels is skewed for the foreseeable future. Schemas are a natural instinct by our brain to make sense of the world as quickly as possible, but it's incredibly easy to take a wrong turn and make your situation worse.

Heuristics. Where schemas help (and hurt) us in learning and interpreting certain things, heuristics are more about how quickly we solve problems and make decisions. A heuristic is a shortcut our minds take when choosing a certain course of action, and as with a schema, it can be helpful or harmful. How do they differ? Where schemas are about understanding a situation at large, heuristics are about your role in a situation and how to act within it. "If this is the situation," a heuristic tells us, "then I should act in this way."

We make hundreds of decisions every day. Most of them are small, ultimately trivial ones: what we'll have for lunch, what radio station we'll listen to on the way home, what grocery store we're going to shop at, and so forth. Unlike major life decisions that could have long-term consequences, we simply can't evaluate every last detail or possible ramification of small decisions. It would be a waste of valuable time and mental energy.

That's where heuristics come in. They're mental guidelines based on past experiences, which we use to make daily decisions that we can't delve deeply into. Think of heuristics as flashcards: they give us quick, abbreviated information to help us make speedy choices about daily decisions that we can't stop and deliberate over. While they're helpful in certain situations in which we need to think more efficiently, heuristics also can work against us by warping our gut instincts and making us lose rationality. For instance, if you've gotten food poisoning three times in the past year, and each time it appeared to be from eating chicken, you will likely formulate a heuristic about avoiding chicken for the foreseeable future. Most commonly, heuristics depend on historical experiences and models.

"Common sense" is an example of a heuristic. If you're a pedestrian standing at a city intersection, the walking signal is showing a red hand, and the traffic in front of you is moving through the street, common sense tells you that you don't want to walk into danger. Hopefully you didn't have to apply a lot of thought to that decision because it was pretty obvious. That's a heuristic. Other heuristics include "rules of thumb" and "educated guesses." They don't require a lot of thought, they're based on things we've known for a while, and they're made quickly. These strategies shorten decision-making time and allow people to function without constantly stopping to think about their next course of action.

There's also the "representativeness heuristic." This is a sort of prototype we use to assess other people or experiences we encounter, which could influence our decision-making. Instead of getting to know a person more deeply, you'd take a look at them, note a few cursory details, and decide what kind of person they are—what they *represent*—based on your what you (think) you already know about people like them.

For example, you might meet someone at work who acts and speaks in a theatrical or dramatic fashion, and you might assume they have some experience in acting or drama. You might decide to ask them to help you do a presentation because they'll be effective in getting a point across (or, possibly, avoid them altogether because they might ham it up).

Heuristics are frequently helpful because we shouldn't ponder too long over every minor choice we have to make, especially in emergency or urgent situations. But there's also a risk of heuristics leading to cognitive bias—i.e., judging based on predetermined ideas rather than the actual situation—or worse.

Another risk is the formation of prejudice and stereotypes. This is particularly perilous when we use heuristics to judge people we come across: we run the risk of making an assumption about them based solely on how they look, dress, or act—or, as happens far too much in the world, strictly on their race or religious beliefs.

We use heuristics, essentially, to save the time and energy of thought—and that's also why they can trigger irrational behavior. As you may have noticed, the running theme of this book is that anything that seeks to cut corners and help you make quicker judgments will eventually be your downfall.

It's fair to use one's experience, recall, memory, and prototypes to make quick decisions, like whether to cross the street or where to get lunch. But they can also trigger irrational thoughts because heuristics are mental shortcuts—they're not designed to take all considerations of a certain situation into account. They can result in irrational behaviors because they're designed to make us think *less*. Instead of getting to know someone who looks different from us, we might form a racist, sexist, or discriminatory opinion of them. Those are bad heuristics.

Intuition is a very important survival instinct, and gut instincts are extremely helpful to ward off disaster in advance. But these instincts are subject to external pressures, and they can also morph into implausible threats and inaction if left unchecked. They're psychological triggers that we need to monitor and evaluate closely so they work in our favor—and, when necessary, stay out of our way.

Cognitive Biases

Cognitive biases are specific flaws in logic or emotion that influence how you process the information right in front of your face. Information that could be plainly obvious to someone else might drive you in the opposite direction because of one of these cognitive decision biases.

Cognitive biases represent flaws in human thinking and, similarly to schemas and heuristics, occur when judgments are made from insufficient information. They are conclusions that we leap to in the absence of, and sometimes in the face of, evidence that says otherwise. You can also think of them as a mental shortcut that seems to make sense at the time but falls apart under deeper scrutiny—the purpose was probably speed and efficiency, but we know what that tends to lead to.

That said, it's very rare that we encounter such scrutiny, so most of us never realize we engage in these biases—and our rational decision-making suffers for it. In fact, many cognitive biases are so robust that they persist even when brought out into the light of day, so they have to be consistently and rationally challenged. For the purposes of illustration, I will be using the same example throughout: deciding between purchasing an expensive, brand-new car and a beat-up older car.

The first cognitive bias that triggers irrational behavior is that humans tend to prefer simplicity. In fact, we believe that something is more accurate the simpler it is. By contrast, we also distrust more complex things. We trust them less and we even become suspicious of them because we feel that decisions should be simple and straightforward. Some decisions *can* be simple, but most of life cannot be reduced to a single question.

In our example, buying a shiny new car is the simple solution. We can trust that it's new, we can see the mileage, and we know it hasn't been crashed before by some shady past owner. We seemingly know what we are getting. We sign, we buy, and we take the car off the lot. It doesn't get simpler than that.

By contrast, buying an older, used car involves exponentially more moving parts—moving parts that could go wrong and that might not be in sync with each other. There are too many factors outside of our control that we aren't able to judge accurately. We always have a sense of suspicion and distrust when buying a used car because we never know how the car has been treated and if we are being told the entire truth. We just don't want to deal.

We prefer simplicity in all walks of life, and that means the decisions that seem the simplest or have the fewest number of moving parts are almost always the ones we'll prefer. They feel more trustworthy, as if everything is transparent.

This also implies another aspect of what we prefer—we favor things that we understand easily and immediately. If we can't, then it's as though there is a logical disconnect and something is being hidden—never mind the fact that many concepts cannot be broken down into something so simple, but that's why this is a cognitive bias.

Psychologists have dubbed this tendency *cognitive fluency*—how easily information is digested and understood. If information is easier to process and more closely resembles a model you already understand and can make a comparison to, it will feel familiar and fluent as a result. For example, studies have found that in the science of branding and marketing, easily pronounceable names and reproducible logos perform far better than others. It's the power of simplicity.

We would love to quickly be able to ascertain the major points of competing decisions, and if we can't, then we mentally write off the more complex version. Just because something is simpler at first glance doesn't mean you should fall for the chance to reduce your due diligence. Sometimes simplicity *is* better, but by itself it means nothing.

The next cognitive bias can be seen very prominently in our example of buying cars. It's the error of being swayed by relative values and relying on contrast rather than independent evaluation. It occurs frequently when you make a comparison to something that doesn't matter yet creates a large contrast, which is not always the metric you should actually be considering.

Let's say the expensive new car you are looking at has a sticker price of $50,000. The used car is only $10,000. However, the new car is currently discounted from the original price of $90,000.

Simply introducing the relative discount sure makes it more attractive, doesn't it? Sometimes we will get caught in this trap of perceived value. It sounds like a good deal to get a $90,000 car for almost half off, but that assumes that the car is actually worth $90,000 and that $50,000 is also a fair price. By introducing the comparison to the number that isn't exactly relevant, one might actually feel that they're getting a steal at $50,000.

However, this isn't considering the car on its own merits or its own absolute value. This is considering it only in comparison to something it shouldn't be compared to: a relative value that makes it appear attractive.

You are stuck on a fundamental misunderstanding of comparisons, not wanting to miss out on something versus evaluating something in a vacuum. True, life doesn't operate in a vacuum, but it's important to keep your focus on the factors that actually matter in your decisions.

In this example, the best course of action would be to judge if the car is actually worth $50,000, despite how much of a discount the price represents. Then you can compare the absolute value of both the new and old cars at their respective price points to make a much better decision that is free of cognitive bias.

If you can't remove yourself from cognitive bias, you just might be fooled into caring about something that is wholly irrelevant to what you are trying to accomplish. When battling the reliance on comparison cognitive bias, try to strip away the fancy trappings and focus on only one factor: the absolute, objective value.

The final cognitive bias I want to touch upon is about the human tendency to avoid all losses. In a way, this cognitive bias could harken back to our more primitive, physiological preference for avoiding pain and uncertainty. In the same way as we might focus more keenly on negative information, we may prioritize perceived losses over gains.

We humans hate to lose things. In fact, we hate to lose things so much that we often would rather not lose anything as opposed to gain a lot. This is referred to as *loss aversion*, and it perfectly encapsulates people's strong tendencies to prefer avoiding loss as opposed to acquiring gains. We build our decisions around the irrational desire to prevent loss, even when it doesn't benefit us very much.

Even if there is a net negative effect from a decision to avoid loss, it psychologically *feels* better and more comfortable than a net positive gain. Emotions are not always useful in highly rational thinking.

Studies by Kahneman and Tversky showed that the motivation, and thus decisional influence, of avoiding losses is twice as powerful as acquiring a gain. If your number-one priority in decisions is to avoid loss, then what happens to the rest of the considerations, which are often more relevant and important? Out the window.

How does this fit into our example of dueling cars, one used and one new? A buyer will buy from whichever salesman is able to make the buyer feel like they own the car as quickly as possible—by putting them in the car, referring to it as theirs, signing papers, or making them otherwise feel emotionally attached. The salesman could even give the car to someone for a thirty-day free trial period, which would really cement the decision for the buyer. This creates the possibility for the feeling of loss we so wish to avoid.

Why is this? When someone gets familiar with a concept or object, especially in as tangible a way as a thirty-day trial, they develop a sense of ownership. Only when you have ownership and attachment does the possibility of loss begin to matter. People usually react with irrational rage over even threatened losses. The act of mentally hearing "It's yours, and I'm taking it away" has a greater effect than hearing "It's here, and I'm taking it away."

How do you think you might react if you thought you had bought the car, only to have it taken away based on a legal technicality? It would be akin to physical pain to part with something you feel is yours.

Loss aversion is a powerful motivation for your irrational decisions, and it causes people to ignore gains to prevent losses, playing it safe in an area when it doesn't actually make sense. The trouble with loss aversion is that it makes you blind to a cost that you don't experience in the present— opportunity cost. This entails everything that you lose by *not* acting, but since you don't feel it there and then, you are likely to write it off.

The pain of losing, or losing out on, something is more salient and raw than the joy from gaining something. We suddenly feel that we have been robbed, which is a stronger emotion than receiving a gift. However, just because the emotions are so disproportionally weighted doesn't mean the path of loss aversion is smarter. The decisions are still equal; negative emotions just tend to take hold of us more strongly and blind us with fear or rage.

Scenario A: I give you $10, then flip a coin. If the coin lands on heads, I take the money back.

Scenario B: I flip a coin. If the coin is a heads, I give you $10.

Which do you prefer?

Scenario B is clearly more comfortable psychologically.

You shouldn't ignore negative consequence in decisions. Just gain awareness that negative consequences have the ability to take root firmly in our brains and never let go. They can emotionally color our perspectives until all we want to do is avoid a slight amount of potential negativity at the expense of a sure positive gain.

Just like heuristics and schemas, cognitive biases are ways in which our brains work too quickly for their own good. A cognitive bias occurs when the brain takes a flawed snapshot of a certain circumstance and instantly makes a judgment. This triggers self-defeating and irrational behaviors, especially these days when advertisers and salespeople are well aware of what motivates people into action.

Wearing Six Hats

It almost seems as if our minds are designed to be triggered into what appears to be the best available option at the moment. Who can blame us for something that seems to make perfect sense on the surface? After all, we're quite selfish, so we don't want to willingly harm ourselves. But how can we resist our so-called instinct and make our good intentions match up with our actions?

Typically, our instincts are designed to fulfill very specific purposes, all related to survival in some respect. Therefore, the key is to take a step back and attempt to view situations and decisions through a different lens. Not survival, not urgency, and sometimes not even happiness. The most prominent technique to achieve this new outlook is called the six hats method.

This technique is extremely thorough and focuses on what humans don't excel at—taking different perspectives. The six hats method is essentially a way to make sure that you're thinking twice and not getting carried away. It presents you with a veritable checklist to run through while you try to make a decision, which ensures that all your bases are covered in terms of rationality, benefits, and cognitive biases. Its power lies in the fact that it is *not* a knee-jerk, unconscious response but a slow, deliberate and considered one.

We've all heard the term that you must wear more than one hat. The six hats method was created by Edward de Bono, and as you might have guessed, it requires looking at a problem or decision from six separate perspectives by wearing six different hats. This gives us an edge when it comes to overcoming unconscious forces, cognitive biases, programmed evolutionary impulses and so on.

Along with the hats themselves, an avatar that embodies the main purpose of each hat will make matters much clearer. It's like you are making a decision by committee, but all the roles are played by you. This is essentially the opposite of thinking with your instincts—you are making sure to uncover all pieces of relevant information and leave no stone unturned. Mature, self-controlled people may do this more naturally, but it's a supremely useful skill that can be learnt and developed by anyone, with time and effort.

The colors of the six hats are white, red, black, yellow, green, and blue. The colors are fairly inconsequential, and it's probably easier if you categorize them by the avatar. I'll go into each of them in depth.

"Tell me more. What does this mean, and where did you get that information?"

The white hat is Sherlock Holmes. This is the thinking and analytical hat. You are trying to gather as much information as possible by whatever means possible. Be observant and act like an information sponge. While you're at it, analyze your information and determine the gaps you have and what you can deduce from what you currently possess. Dig deep, fill in the information gaps, and try to gather an understanding of what you really have in front of you.

You want to absorb as much of the available information as you can while also determining what you are missing to make a more informed and more perfect decision. The white hat is also where you should be resourceful about learning. As we discussed earlier, lack of information is one of the worst detriments to your decisions.

Make sure you are armed with information, that you seek multiple perspectives and don't let yourself be influenced by bias. You want an objective view of the entire landscape. Get out your magnifying glass and start sleuthing, Detective Holmes.

"And how does that make you feel? Why is that?"

The red hat is Sigmund Freud, the psychotherapist. This is your emotion hat. You are trying to determine how you feel about something and what your gut tells you. Those are not always the same emotions. Combined with the information you collected as Sherlock Holmes, this will already give you a more complete picture than you are used to.

You are asking how you feel about your options and why. Beyond the objective level, decisions affect us on an emotional plane. You must account for that—happiness and unhappiness. Ask yourself what you find yourself leaning toward or avoiding and why that might be. You can also attempt to predict how others might react emotionally. Your actions might have consequences beyond your current understanding, and how people will feel is often different from how you think they will feel. What are the origins of your emotions toward each option, and are they reasonable or even relevant, for that matter? Often, our emotions aren't in the open, so when you can uncover them, you will understand your options better.

"I don't know. I have my doubts. What about X? Will Y really happen that way?"

The black hat is Eeyore, the morose donkey from *Winnie the Pooh*. If you don't know who that is, you can imagine the black hat to be the ultimate depressed pessimist that never believes anything will work out. Indeed, the purpose of the black hat is to attempt to poke holes in everything and to try to account for everything that can go wrong. They are skeptics who always look on the darker side of life.

They believe in *Murphy's law*: everything that can go wrong *will* go wrong. This is a hat most people never wear because they are afraid to look at their decisions, or reasoning, from a critical point of view. On some level, it probably indicates recognition that their views fall apart under deeper scrutiny, but that is exactly why it's so important to wear the black hat.

It's essentially planning for failure and the worst-case scenario. Planning for success is easy and instantaneous, but what happens when things don't work out and you have to put out fires? How would you plan differently if you thought there was a high probability of failure?

You change your approach, look for alternatives, and create contingency plans to account for everything. This is the type of analysis that leads to better planning and decisions because you can objectively take into account what is good and what is not. Wearing your black hat makes your plans tougher and stronger over the long haul, though it can be exhausting to continually reject positivity and hopefulness.

"It's going to be so great when this all comes together. Just imagine how you'll feel."

The yellow hat is the cheerleader. It is the opposite of the black hat—you are now thinking positively and optimistically. This is a motivating hat that allows you to feel good about your decision and the value of putting all the work into it. This is where you turn dark clouds into a silver lining.

It also allows you to project into the future and imagine the opportunities that come along with it. If this decision goes well, what else will follow? Where do optimistic projections place you, and what is necessary for you to reach them?

Belief in yourself is still one of the concepts that fuels achievement and motivation, so it's important to balance a positive outlook with pessimism and nitpicking flaws.

"Call me crazy, but what if we completely change X and try Y?"

The green hat is Pablo Picasso, the famous artist. This hat is for creativity. When you wear this hat, you want to think outside the box and come up with creative perspectives, angles, and solutions to whatever you are facing. It can be as simple as pretending that your current leading option is unavailable and having to figure out what you can do instead. You have to deviate from the current options and discover other ways of solving your problem.

Brainstorming is the name of the game here. No judgment or criticism is allowed when you are wearing this hat because you want to generate as many ideas as possible. You can always curate them later, but the more solutions you can think of, no matter how zany or ineffective, there will always be something you can learn or apply from them.

This is also a hat of open-mindedness and not being stuck in one track of thinking, which can be dangerous if you refuse to alter your course in the face of hardships.

"Now, now, children. Everyone will have their turn to be heard."

The blue hat is Henry Ford, founder of Ford Motor Company and inventor of the modern assembly line. The blue hat is all about coordinating and creating a system to integrate all the information you obtained from the other hats. You can also look at this hat as the CEO hat: you are in charge of making things happen and putting things in place, though not necessarily in charge of creating anything by yourself.

Your responsibility is to weigh how heavily each hat should be considered and what factors you must take into account when integrating the information. The CEO knows the context the best, so the input from each different hat is synthesized and weighed based on personal priorities and the situation at hand. You are the ultimate decider.

Now that you know how each hat functions, it's time to illustrate how they all work together. Let's suppose you are considering buying a new house.

Wearing the white Sherlock hat, you would examine all the information you have about the current market. That wouldn't be enough, so you would conduct far more independent research on the economy and market trends and come up with a clear sense of how much it will cost you, where you will live in the meantime, and if you are okay with the long-term tradeoff.

You would want prices on everything, data on past prices, predictions on future prices, and the other benefits and drawbacks to living in the new house. Then you'd take all that data and compare it to your current living situation, as well as to other houses in the area.

Wearing the red Freud hat, you would introspect and determine how you feel about the new house emotionally and intuitively. Will it make you happy regardless of the cost? What does your gut tell you? Money certainly can't buy happiness, but it can set the stage for it. Is the new house going to help with that? Are you drained by this process or energized by it? Recall that the red hat suggests you think about the emotional impact your decision will have.

Wearing the pessimistic Eeyore black hat, you would try to plan for the worst-case scenario for before and after you buy this new house—for example, if the market tanks and the house drops in value by half or if you lose your job and have to relocate to a new city far away from your new house. In a darker turn, you might lose your job and not be able to find a new one, meaning you'd be saddled with a mortgage that you can't pay.

What other factors inside or outside of your control might make purchasing a new house a terrible decision? The construction might be faulty, the previous owner might have lied to you, and the neighbors might be horrible. Plan for them so you can account for them.

Wearing the optimistic cheerleader yellow hat, what is the best-case scenario for purchasing a new house and how will that affect and benefit your life? Perhaps the house will increase twofold in value in the next three years, and perhaps you will be able to sell it for a huge profit while still living in the area. It might be a house for your family, so you'll feel stable and secure while in a good school district. Do these outweigh any potential negatives?

Despite all the problems for the new house, it might be nicer than anything you've ever lived in, and it represents a dream come true for you. Worst-case scenario, you can always rent a room to your cousin.

Wearing the Picasso green hat of creativity, you can think of additional ways to solve your problem of wanting to live in a new place. For example, would you sleep on a friend's couch to see if you need a big house? Rent a monthly house in the area first before committing to purchasing? Put in a new stove in your current house and find you won't have to move? What other areas of the city do you want to explore and live in? How else can you invest the money in a safe and smart way? Do you actually want to live in a new home, or do you have other desires?

When you get to the blue Henry Ford hat, your job is to sort through all the information you've uncovered, try to decide what is really important, and use it to make the most informed decision of your life. Perhaps you've decided that the money is simply too tight for a new house, and what you really wanted was to have a nicer kitchen. Or perhaps you've found that the housing market is at an all-time low, so even if you are low on money, it would be one of the best financial decisions to immediately take the leap.

The point of the six hats method is to take a deep dive into a particular perspective and temporarily tune everything else out. Give one direction free rein and reject all opposition to it for the time being. That's just about the only way you will be able to make a compelling argument for something that you don't wholeheartedly believe in at first. You want to embody the hat you currently wear and have a debate with yourself, moderated by the blue hat.

If you are being purely driven by just one or two of these perspectives, your view is necessarily limited—and you may well make mistakes or miss crucial information. By slowing down and taking your time to explore all these different aspects, you are essentially overcoming the biases of being just one person with a single viewpoint.

The hats represent your interests. You'll be able to see clearly which interests of yours you have focused on in the past. There might be interests that you don't prioritize as much as others, but they are your interests regardless. It's all a process to make sure that your top interests win out in the end (if they deserve to). On the other hand, it's also a great way to make sure you're not unconsciously ignoring some crucial perspective that may have ultimately caused you to behave differently had you considered it.

To summarize, the six hats method of thinking implores you to view a fork in the road from six distinct perspectives. Typically, these are represented by colors, but avatars are more illustrative. The six different perspectives to consider are Sherlock Holmes (gather information), Sigmund Freud (emotions), Eeyore the donkey (pessimist), a cheerleader (optimist), Pablo Picasso (creativity), and Henry Ford (information synthesis).

Psychological triggers thrive on confusion, misinformation, and a race against the clock. Our instincts evolved in an attempt to battle these factors, and while they may work from time to time, the age of urgency is gone in lieu of the age of consequences. In other words, instincts, hunches, and gut feelings can easily lead you astray into irrationality, even when it feels right.

Takeaways:
- Our instincts have kept us alive thus far. Overall, it may be beneficial to have an "act first, think later" approach to life. But many of those actions and behaviors

will inevitably be irrational or harmful because you are inherently acting with incomplete or imperfect information. So what do you do? Ignore what your gut tells you? Yes and no.

- Our gut feelings are formed largely by two psychological concepts: schemas and heuristics. Schemas are mental shortcuts that define our conception of a certain situation ("Based on what I see, what is happening here?") while heuristics are mental shortcuts that inform our place and role in certain situations ("Based on what I see, what should I be doing right now?"). They both work to eliminate decisions from your mental workload, but this isn't always beneficial. They are largely subconscious and can lead to skewed realities if left uncorrected.

- Cognitive biases are additional ways our brain's propensity for shortcuts can harm us. They are errors in thinking that we struggle to see because our brains prefer to move ahead and ask questions later. Here, we only cover a few cognitive biases, though there are literally hundreds: preference for simplicity, reliance on contrast, and loss aversion.

- Finally, what can we do to battle these instincts that occasionally help us but harm us more often than not? Enter the six hats method of thinking, which encourages us to literally think about a situation or problem from six different perspectives. The creator, Edward de Bono, used colors, but avatars are a bit more helpful: Sherlock Holmes (gather information), Sigmund Freud (emotions), Eeyore the donkey (pessimist), a cheerleader (optimist), Pablo Picasso (creativity), and Henry Ford (information synthesis).

Chapter 6. Free Will and Control

There is a final series of psychological triggers that's a bit different from most of the others we've discussed so far. Up to this point, we've talked about the social environment we inhabit, the raw power of emotions, and even natural human drives and instincts that can push us from calm thinking into outrageous behaviors.

So why is this chapter different? It's about the triggers that spring from our need to believe we're in control of our own destinies. Hate to break it to you, but in large part we're not. Not even me. And it drives us crazy. Even me.

These triggers aren't necessarily products of our biological makeup or evolutionary instincts—they are, in many ways, brain oddities that were more profoundly shaped in the course of our becoming civilized. They didn't necessarily help keep us alive, but rather, the need to feel control and free will kept us sane and comfortable where we would otherwise have been in constant tension with the world.

What exactly is this thought that makes us feel comfortable with our small and insignificant place in the world? We need to believe that we have power to affect every outcome and control every situation—at least, that we aren't powerless and completely at the whim of chance and random occurrences. It drives us crazy to realize that the world is not, in fact, hinging on our every decision.

Occasionally, we get reminders of this feeling in our daily lives. When we feel powerless against circumstances in our lives—a breakup, a problem at work—the realization of how little we control our situations can be overwhelming. Knowing how insignificant we are in the grand scheme of things is a disturbing, unsettling realization to make. The feeling of lacking control is a dreary catalyst for irrational behavior.

Humans have developed beliefs to cope with that hopelessness, and that trigger makes us act out in irrational ways and make unusual choices.

You don't need to look much further than your own habits to confirm the notion that we love the illusion of control. Do you feel that things go better when you engage in acts that are completely unrelated to them? For example, do you only watch your favorite sports teams with your jersey on, or do you need a certain pair of pants for when you give speeches?

If so, then you're engaging in irrational thinking in pursuit of the feeling of control!

Superstitions in general are irrational belief systems born out of that pursuit for control. When bad things happen to good people, as they say, they search for reasons why these troubles come down on them. Many times, there isn't a direct cause: sickness, natural disasters, death, and hardship are often just fateful events that nobody forced upon a person on purpose. But that answer's not sufficient for many people—they absolutely must feel there's some aspect that they can control or influence. And that gives rise to beliefs that have no basis in fact but make people feel like there's something they can also do to change their luck.

So they avoid walking under ladders because doing so is supposed to bring bad luck, they interpret dreams as fortune-telling, or they stay safely at home on Friday the 13th. None of these techniques have any foundation in scientific or historical truth, but they provide the illusion that we can do something (or *not* do something) to spur the arrival of good luck and discourage the coming of bad luck. On paper, this looks like irrational behaviors triggered by a desire for control. That's because they are.

Superstition

Who among us will openly admit they believe in the supernatural? People might not willingly claim they believe in ghosts and monsters under the bed, but nonetheless, the vast majority of people have been shown to possess some sort of superstitious routines.

Want your favorite sports team to win? You might just feel better if you wear the same pair of socks you wore the last time they won. These habits creep into our lives in small, almost imperceptible ways that make it second nature for us to believe in their power.

Essentially, *the supernatural* has become a catch-all umbrella term for things that lack a conventional explanation. Can't explain it? Must be something supernatural. There may not always be a clear explanation, but blaming the missing cookies on a ghost and not the dog belies a very interesting tendency for humans to try to apply understanding to that which is out of their grasp.

You've likely read about this tendency when learning about ancient and not-so-ancient civilizations. The Greeks assigned a god to nearly everything as a scapegoat or savior, and Native Americans engaged in rain dances to help their crops flourish for the coming harvest. The Mayans carried out ritual human sacrifice to appease their gods and seek good fortune. We have the overwhelming desire to feel in control; if we are out of control, then we risk feeling insignificant or subject to danger. When we feel we have control over something, we are suddenly more engaged and invested; if we think there is no control, we feel helpless to the powers that be.

We believe in supernatural forces exerting control because the existence of something we don't understand, yet can blame, is far more comforting than no explanation at all. Humans just don't like to feel that we are random molecules of carbon and hydrogen that happened to coalesce and form somehow—we might be, but it sure feels better if we have a purpose.

Superstitions are the main way we tend to put our faith into the unknown to feel like we aren't just waiting for random occurrences to dictate our lives.

Superstitions are behaviors or thought patterns that people engage in because there is the belief of a cause-and-effect relationship. You engage in superstitious acts because you believe it will get you closer to a specific outcome. For instance, if you notice that your favorite football team has won the past three times you've worn red underwear, a new superstition will be born: red underwear only on game days. You might not affect the game itself, but there appears to be a pattern of causation, so you're going to adhere to it—sometimes even subconsciously.

Classical conditioning is the cause for many superstitions we hold throughout our lives. We commit an act, we see an outcome, and we begin to link the two, even though it's no more than a correlation or simple coincidence. Surprisingly to some sports fans, sitting in the same chair while watching matches likely does not affect the end outcome just because it happened twice three years ago. This is why people don't walk under ladders, because negative occurrences have coincided with that event—never mind the fact that walking under a ladder puts you directly into the path of falling debris.

Illogical as they may be, these beliefs are what humans have the tendency to cling to. Pigeons, as the famous psychologist B.F. Skinner proved in 1948, exhibit similar behavior. During his study, he found pigeons learned to continue behaviors that coincided with food appearing, despite the food appearing at set intervals. In other words, pigeons saw patterns that produced an outcome they wanted and kept doing it, even though there was no causal relationship.

Shana Wilson from Kent State University investigated why people, specifically sports fans, engage in superstitious behavior. The study concluded that people who engage in superstitious behaviors are more susceptible to what is called the *uncertainty hypothesis*, which is the idea that when people feel a complete lack of certainty, they seek to find a way in which they feel they can exert some degree of control over it. A lack of certainty is extremely uncomfortable and unsettling, and being able to point to something as a cause eases the underlying tension.

We can find examples of this in our own daily lives. We all hate bumper-to-bumper traffic. We enjoy driving unimpeded to our destinations. Which would you prefer: bumper-to-bumper traffic or driving unimpeded, both of which would culminate in you driving the same distance over the same amount of time? Most of us would choose the latter; we would choose to travel without obstacles because we can control the speed of our car and how slowly or quickly we go. Being stuck in a situation like bumper-to-bumper traffic, where we have zero control and are subject to the infernal gods of traffic, gives us feelings of hopelessness and helplessness.

Not having control over situations, at the extreme end of the spectrum, is a feeling that underlies types of anxiety and depression. What motivation could you possibly have if you were certain everything would turn out terribly, despite your efforts? Therefore, many times, the more important an uncontrollable situation is, the more likely people will try to exert a measure of control through superstitious behavior.

Superstitions are generally harmless, unless they replace actual work and effort. Problems arise when people can't distinguish between an outcome they can control and an outcome that is beyond their control. Unfortunately, this is exactly what causes irrational behaviors—when a ritual or behavior has zero hope of affecting change, yet we still adhere to it religiously. Sometimes our superstitions can be downright harmful, especially when we rely upon them.

Stuart Vyse, author and professor at Connecticut College, chalks superstitious behaviors up to the comforts of illusory control, saying, "There is evidence that positive, luck-enhancing superstitions provide a psychological benefit that can improve skilled performance. There is anxiety associated with the kinds of events that bring out superstition. The absence of control over an important outcome creates anxiety. So, even when we know on a rational level that there is no magic, superstitions can be maintained by their emotional benefit. Furthermore, once you know that a superstition applies, people don't want to tempt fate by not employing it."

Positive superstitions can improve confidence and reduce anxiety because they are the panacea to all that ails you. If you are shy about a job interview and you always wear lucky socks during job interviews, you are going in with a head full of confidence because you feel you are complete and fully armed for battle. This is positive and can be helpful in providing a psychological advantage over not having any superstitious behaviors at all. These help us complete the self-fulfilling prophecy where if we think we are (because of a superstitious behavior, anyway), then we are.

Superstitions are extremely easy to acquire, and they are likely more widespread than you realize. Our brains are fooling us into a sense of illusory control because it feels more comfortable that way. However, that comfort sometimes distorts reality in very detrimental and irrational ways.

Why Do We See Faces in Toast?

With superstitions and magical thinking, you have the symptoms of a brain struggling to feel safe and secure. In doing so, the brain tries to fill in the gaps from the incomplete information it received from the world. We can see the brain's tendency to overcompensate to the point of skewing reality, and perhaps the epitome of this tendency is *pareidolia*: seeing visual patterns in randomness where none exist.

Pareidolia, in simpler terms, is seeing an image of Jesus in a piece of toast or picking out formations in clouds as animals. You have probably experienced pareidolia many times, though you may have not realized what your brain was actually doing. The brain is so powerful it is capable of merging information you have stored with incoming signals to find even more patterns; when the brain starts recognizing patterns in what is actually just random noise, this is pareidolia.

Pareidolia stems from the fact that as rational beings, we have a desire to make sense of the world. We want things to fit into identifiable categories and for different categories to have clear relationships with one another. In the case of pareidolia, our brains are simply confused by the signals they receive, and we identify patterns and correlations that do not exist in an attempt to find understanding.

This can lead us to believe that we have seen things that do not actually exist. For example, consider the life of a Wall Street investor. Investors are notorious for trying to find patterns within the random noise of the stock market. Some use complex algorithms and computer simulations to try to predict the market. Others study the complex information presented in financial reports, and then they try to determine which companies are poised for the biggest gains. Either way, having a good view of the market and stocks is the first step. Then investors must make a decision.

Without quality information and models, the investor would have no idea which stocks were set to increase. This uncertainty would make the investor's job impossible, as investing would become an extremely risky gamble. The investor would likely just throw their hands in the air, fully defeated by their lack of information.

Our brains operate like a stock investor, constantly analyzing our surroundings, building models, and trying to predict the outcomes. This allows us to accurately predict the outcomes of our actions, protect ourselves from known dangers, find ways to benefit ourselves, and create an opening for a wide variety of other behaviors. But just like the stock investor can create a bad model that sees false patterns, so too can our brains find false patterns among all the noise. The fact is, there are not always ghost patterns in what we experience. Some stock investors go bankrupt because they see things that aren't there. Some things are indeed just random chaos.

Perception is an active process within your mind that is constantly trying to incorporate the outside world into familiar mental models. If you close your eyes and imagine a spoon, your ideal model of a spoon will be presented based on your experiences. When you see a spoon you have never seen before, your brain takes this information and incorporates it into your existing model of a spoon.

But what happens when you see an unknown object? Your brain is still going to try to classify the information, so it will compare it to everything it knows. If the object is elongated and metal and has a cupped end, your brain might decide that this is another spoon. In fact, your brain is so adept at this process that it will sometimes ignore or avoid certain aspects of the object to fit it within an existing category. This is like shoving a square peg into a round hole.

One of the most common times pareidolia happens is when our minds try to recognize a face within an inanimate object. This happens all the time. Even the yellow, simplified "smiley face" is a great example. This common symbol has no nose, eyebrows, skin, hair, or any other feature that would let us know it is human. Yet when two black dots are placed above a curved line on a yellow circle, we instantly see a smiling face. This is known as facial pareidolia, and like other forms of pareidolia, it likely has its roots in evolutionary history.

Pareidolia is a subset of a greater phenomenon known as *apophenia,* which is the general process of interpreting false patterns from data. This phenomenon can also happen with information we consume, feelings we experience, or even numbers and words that we hear. Recall that pareidolia only occurs when we have found false patterns within the images we see.

Further, pareidolia appears to be largely related to our ability to recognize faces and other objects within our natural environment. For obvious reasons, it has always been important that humans and their ancestors can find food, hide from predators, and recognize their family and friends. Imagine what would have happened to any caveman without these abilities. He would likely be eaten by the first wild animal that he failed to recognize as dangerous. Even if he managed to avoid the wildlife, he would still be lost in a world where he could not tell what tribe he belonged to or who his relatives were.

In fact, famous astronomer and physicist Carl Sagan hypothesized that pareidolia is an overextension of our ability to recognize faces. Sagan succinctly summarized his theory as "Those infants who a million years ago were unable to recognize a face smiled back less, were less likely to win the hearts of their parents, and less likely to prosper."

This ability to recognize a face is a complex process within the brain that analyzes all of the structures and patterns within a human face. Just like your ideal image of a spoon, you have an idealized image of a face. Through trial and error, you learn which of these patterns are faces and which are not. When we interpret a yellow circle with two black dots and a curved line as a face, this is the simplest version of that pattern recognition.

In a sense, we all have a certain degree of facial pareidolia that was necessary for our ancestors to develop bonds and care for each other. As such, people with the ability to discern faces were more likely to survive and more likely to produce offspring. This increased the trait within the human population, and now, like most traits that allowed us to survive in harsh conditions, they are more hindrances than help.

Reactance Theory

This is another trigger that directly stems from our lack of control and attempts to deal with it.

Reactance theory originated from Jack Brehm in 1966. It is a theory that dictates how humans behave when they feel their free will or freedom is being threatened. As a simple example, this is what children feel when they are told they can't jump on the bed or climb the ladder. If you've ever been around kids, what do you suppose might happen after admonishing them? They'll develop an even bigger appetite for what was supposed to be forbidden. Humans will bristle when their perceived freedom is restricted, so they'll try to reclaim it. It is similar to reverse psychology, and the mental dialogue sounds something like "Who says I can't? Now I'm going to show you that I can!"

In other words, if we are told we can't do something, we immediately want to do it— not because of the action itself, but because we feel psychological discomfort with being told we can't do something, and we seek to prove to ourselves that we indeed can. We will probably have a more urgent desire to perform that action if we are told we can't do it because it will have greater psychological and emotional value at that point.

So for instance, if you are told you can't buy something, you are likely to feel slighted and annoyed at the fact someone told you this. You might even feel insulted or controlled. All of these emotions lead to you buying something you may not want just to resolve those negative feelings inside you and be able to say, "Ha, I showed them!"

We can accept some restrictions on our freedom. We abide by them all the time, from not crossing the street at red lights to not stealing. The difference is, these rules are universally applied and generally appear to be reasonable and fair. Reactance theory kicks in most powerfully when we feel our freedom is unfairly, arbitrarily, or unreasonably restricted—in our perception.

Reactance theory shows an interesting aspect of the human desire for choice and options. Choice and options give us the feeling that we can control what happens in our lives.

In 1976, Pennebaker and Sanders studied reactance and illustrated it in a somewhat humorous way. They didn't give instruction to participants directly. Instead, they put two types of signs up in bathrooms. One sign read, "Do not write on these walls under any circumstances," while the other sign contained no such language.

Can you guess what happened?

The signs with language specifically prohibiting writing were covered with graffiti, while the normal signs had far less or none at all. What people were specifically told to avoid, they did to satiate an impulse they had about their freedom. I imagine the inner monologue of someone who came across that sign was something like, "Oh yeah? Stupid sign creator trying to tell me what to do? I'll show them." It may sound immature, but it was a textbook instance of a seemingly unreasonable restriction on free will that caused people to demonstrate their free will.

There probably weren't many graffiti artists in the area, but the people who drew on the signs just wanted to feel that they could without anyone running into the bathroom and arresting them. They had the power, and they weren't going to be told what to do by a *sign*.

Reactance theory might also be behind one of literature's greatest love stories: *Romeo and Juliet*. How else might teenagers act if they were explicitly told to not see someone because their families were feuding?

Whatever the case, reactance theory is more commonly utilized as reverse psychology. Tell people to do something, and intend for them to do the opposite. Tell someone she can't sleep, and watch her to do the opposite. Tell someone he can't possibly buy that shirt, and he probably will. Tell your significant other they are forbidden from looking inside your desk, and they *definitely* will.

Knowing this is the case, you can convince people to do what you want by insinuating they don't have the freedom to do the opposite. Specifically, if you want action X, you can imply or outright state any of the following:

- They can't do X.
- They are forbidden from doing X.
- They are incapable of doing X.
- They aren't allowed to do X.
- They can't handle X.
- Trust me, you don't want to do X.

- X isn't for people like you.

How would *you* react to any of those subtle jabs? I can guarantee you wouldn't agree outright, and there would absolutely be varying degrees of resistance, annoyance, and anger. This is reactance theory in a nutshell. We can be spiteful creatures from time to time. It also capitalizes on other aspects of human nature, such as curiosity, excitement about forbidden fruit, and rising to meet a challenge.

Reactance theory is a strong reflection of how much people value their freedom of choice. It can trigger people into doing things that are directly detrimental to them—just to demonstrate and show off free will and control.

How to Deal with Having No Control

Uncertainty is terribly uncomfortable and scary. But why? Why do so many of us work so hard to stay in control and know what's going on at all times? It comes down to our fear of the unknown, which is a huge source of psychological triggers. It's human nature to look at anything new, anything unknown or strange or out of the ordinary as a potential threat. This makes sense: if something novel pops up in your world, it could be *anything*—and that includes something potentially terrifying.

While there is a huge cost to failing to recognize a threat to safety, there isn't the same cost to failing to recognize a potential good thing. The "unknown" may turn out to be something that greatly improves our lives—but then, if that's the case, we needn't have done anything to prepare for it. This sets up a sort of bias where we zoom in on the unknown and frame it in terms of its potential negatives. We are hardwired for bad news, and also to "fear the unknown."

This may be why many of us equate uncertainty with bad scenarios—things being forgotten or overlooked, poor planning being exploited—and we do everything we can to make our lives orderly and predictable. We try to mitigate stressful feelings by making the unknown smaller and more manageable. We force conclusions where there aren't any or take actions that only *feel* like they put us more in charge. Truly controlling everything is, of course, impossible; the only thing that's certain in life is, indeed, uncertainty.

Learning how to deal with the prospect of uncertainty is therefore important, because it helps us deal with the irrational thoughts and behaviors that come from our lack of control. Curiously, it's sometimes our inability to tolerate uncertainty and ambiguity that is most uncomfortable—when we can "sit with" the unknown, we give it a chance to be filled with potential and possibility, rather than simply fearing and avoiding it.

Recall how absolutely insane you can become in a dating scenario where you're receiving mixed signals from your potential prospect—do they or don't they like you? You'll want to seek certainty one way or another, and this will cause you to keep in touch far too often, to say the least. There are a few steps we can take that can help us endure those periods of awful suspense without resorting to superstition, rubbing crystals, or relying upon the concept of universal *karma*.

Let it go. That Disney heroine was right: the first action you need to take in the face of uncertainty is to grit your teeth and accept the situation as it is. This assertion runs exactly counter to your embedded need to control everything. This is not an action you need to take so much as a recognition for how things *already are.* What you are letting go of is your *illusion* of control. Realizing you only have so much under your command and agreeing to tolerate unsure circumstances goes a very long way toward restoring a measure of calm.

A big area in which letting go is important involves the plans we've made for ourselves. We get so wrapped up in what we most desire—the perfect job, a healthy bank account, problem-free friendships and relationships, a life of endless travel—that the prospect of never obtaining these goals debilitates us and makes us feel like failures.

Letting go of those far-off dreams doesn't mean you won't ever achieve them—but it will free you up to focus on what needs to be done in the here and now to keep your life moving along. It helps you appreciate what you have, something you can call up on a daily basis. Finally, it can help open us up to potentials and possibilities we missed while we were so hell-bent on what we thought was the only way forward. Those sentiments help us adjust to situations where we feel we've lost control.

Visualize the positive. Staring into the abyss of the unknown conjures up our fears about how everything can go horribly, horribly wrong. It's an all-consuming and nauseating thought. But often those fears are unfounded, and as we've seen, exaggerated. We tend to exaggerate the possibility of bad outcomes and misjudge the likelihood of failure, all while forgetting that the unknown may in fact hold something wonderful for us, or that change may be for the better. To combat those worries, visualize a positive result—your best-case scenario. Imagine how it will feel to accomplish exactly what you're after and hold on to that picture.

For example, some athletes use deep visualization tactics to picture themselves winning a championship—how it feels to finish the game or race, the celebrations that come afterward, and the sweet afterglow of victory. It's not too hard to see how we can emulate that visualization in our lives: picture yourself finishing your book and seeing it become a best-seller. Or imagine yourself owning a small retail business, with customers coming in around the clock, and you enjoying the fruits of financial independence. Keeping a positive overview of the big picture will help power us through the lesser situations we can't control and keep us on the path of rationality and not hasty decisions.

Reflect on the past. Surely you've been through periods of uncertainty before. Judging from your current circumstance, you appear to have come out alive. But we tend to forget that we've done so in times of doubt, and a phenomenon known as "hindsight bias" makes us believe, quite mistakenly, that everything that happened to us before now was always a matter of certainty. It wasn't. So take a few minutes to reflect on those times and what got you through them, and take some cues from your thoughts to help you push through now.

Remind yourself that you have tolerated uncertainty in the past and that, even when you didn't necessarily feel in control at the time, things nevertheless turned out OK. Remind yourself that it's OK to act without complete knowledge or take a leap even when you're a little unsure—after all, haven't you done it with great success before? Remind yourself, also, that it's OK to be *in process*—as long as you are learning something new or becoming better in some way, there's going to be a learning curve and it's not always going to be convenient, easy or simple along the way.

For example, you might currently be under- or unemployed. You may feel stuck in an immobile state and don't think you'll ever get out of it again. You might think your chances are all used up, which is baseless speculation as it is. But think back to the last time you achieved something momentous and how much work you had to do to get to that point. It wasn't automatically bestowed—you had to struggle and focus to get it done. Whether it was getting the lead role in a school play, finishing a tough college course with good grades, closing a lucrative business deal with outside partners, or just making the perfect tuna casserole, there was a point when you did *not* have that experience, and then there was a point when you *did*. Remember how you had to work at it and how well it turned out.

Don't do nothing. Uncertainty can be crippling. But it can also be energizing if you let it. Our stimulated nervous system gets into action, and it can help us take measures to effect at least a little progress. That's much better than allowing ourselves to get hamstrung with doubt. Try to push yourself to keep moving and deal with what's coming directly—stop avoiding the problem and get out in front of it. Uncertainty can send your brain into endless machinations, or you can use that same energy to fix what you're uncertain about.

For example, you might be terrified of failing at a certain endeavor—let's say, a freelance writing job. The anxiety of that uncertainty causes some people to snap into work mode, but it turns others into dead weight, unable to navigate their fear or protect themselves. But they can always do something: the writer can keep writing, which might generate more ideas and keep them going.

Understand what's possible. Uncertainty is actually an opportunity for a fresh start. *Something* can happen. At one point you took action so that you'd get to the place where you are now—on the cusp of new chances and possible fortunes. You're in a position to write your next chapter and set future plans into effect. When you switch your perspective from fear to prospects, you might make the eventual outcome easier to handle—and, maybe, even help it become positive. There are two ends of the spectrum that come with uncertainty, and you are only fixating on the negative one.

For example, say your company's reorganized and you're nervous as to what the end result might mean for your career—will you be reassigned to a position you don't like or even get laid off? This is a situation that rightly scares almost everyone who faces it.

And yet, some people are able to power through this situation in which they have no control. If they're reassigned, they have a new chance to prove themselves to another supervisor.

They may be able to chart their own course for a fresh set of eyes. They can even find a way to make being laid off something other than a worst-case scenario. They can work on their own business ideas or take some much-needed time off to relax or accept a job from a competitor. There's nothing so dire about this situation that it contains no positive possibilities whatsoever—there's always something beneficial. By concentrating on how they can execute that pivot in the future, this person lessens the blow of the current reality they have no control over.

There's a lot in this existence that is hopelessly out of our hands. But our perception of lack of control as a state of adversity can be overblown, and sometimes the illusions of free will and control become snares in our thinking. Learning the right way to release our expectations and exist in the moment will help lessen the psychological triggers that happen when we discover we can't control everything—which should be a liberating realization.

We actually can't control whether our sports team wins, whether it rains, or whether we hit all green lights on the drive home from work. Accepting this will keep us on the straight and narrow and away from self-defeating and time-wasting behaviors.

Takeaways:

- The final set of psychological triggers that cause us to act irrationally are the human notions of free will and control over our destinies. What of it? Well, we like to feel that we have those things, even though we realistically don't. Our lives are more accurately deemed a set of random occurrences, opportunities, and chances. But that doesn't stop us from engaging in irrational behaviors that are detrimental, harmful, and self-defeating—all in the hope of gaining at most the illusion of control.

- Superstitions are the best example of wanting to gain the illusion of control. What won't we do for our favorite sports team to win? We go to great lengths with some of our rituals because we feel less tension with the world when it seems like we can affect outcomes or events.

- *Pareidolia* is the human tendency to see faces (i.e. patterns) where they don't exist. It's an extension of our natural desire to understand and make meaning of the world, as well as to control, predict and master it. Our brains are always actively interpreting sense experiences and incoming data from the surrounding environment, often drawing conclusions and seeing connections or patterns that aren't actually there—something to be aware of if we wish to remain objective!

- Reactance theory is similar to reverse psychology. If you restrict someone's freedom or free will, they will feel triggered to demonstrate their agency to you. "Jane told me I can't do this, so I'm going to do it in front of her face." It's a powerful draw.

- So how do we deal with this lack of control in the universe? Are we to just accept that good things happen to bad people while bad things happen to good people, that there is no sense of cosmic justice and we are just a set of molecules and atoms that happen to be birthed into bodies? Yes and no. Acceptance is certainly part of the answer to keep you from acting irrationally in the pursuit of the illusion of control. But so is letting go, making sure not to give in to inaction, reflecting on past occurrences, and thinking through positive possibilities.

Summary Guide

- What are psychological triggers? Put simply, they are what drive our behavior far more than we would care to admit or even think about. We are slaves to our impulses—and for most of us, this manifests in horribly negative ways.

- Triggers stem from evolutionary risk detection, which means that we have evolved to avoid pain and seek pleasure. We may not even realize what we are doing and may be unable to point out what pain and pleasure we are orienting ourselves around. Our impulses kept us alive in prior days but are wholly unsuited for the modern age.

- The best example of this phenomenon is phobias, which are irrational fears of benign harms—for instance, being afraid of heights, spiders, or deep water. Objectively, they are not directly harmful to you, but there's something primal, deep inside of us, that makes us react. What powers all of these triggers thus far? Fear and anxiety—possibly the most universal and predictable psychological trigger in the world. Where fear exists, you can count on irrational behavior, because fear makes us want to act quickly, not intelligently or effectively.

- If psychological triggers are so commonplace and frequent, to what degree are we actually acting out of free will? Are we choosing our own lives, or are we just a complex set of impulses and influences? When you take into account fear, along with Freud's concept of the subconscious, with a dash of Skinner's reliance on the environment, it becomes clear that acting out of free will is the exception rather than the rule.

CHAPTER 2. SOCIAL TRIGGERS

- The people around us aren't just sources of companionship—they are one of the most powerful sources of influence and psychological triggers! It may not be conscious, and it may not even be peer pressure, but we almost never make decisions in a social vacuum, and this often has negative consequences. We are pressured to conform, we bend to displays of authority, and we fulfill the roles and labels we are given.

- Three seminal psychological studies showed how susceptible we are to social influence: the Asch conformity study, the Milgram shock study, and the Stanford prison experiment. How can we truly claim to be acting out of free will when shocking evidence exists otherwise?

- Theorists like Le Bon, McDougall and Freud saw crowd behavior as a powerful psychological trigger. Their theories characterized group behavior as irrational, emotionally driven, "primitive" and a means to release latent unconscious desires. More modern theorists such as Allport, however, concede that crowd behavior can actually serve a social function.

- The ideomotor effect suggests that people can unconsciously and involuntarily behave in ways so as to bring about expected or anticipated results—for example, subtly moving the Ouija board planchette themselves but sincerely believing that someone else (or a spirit!) moved it. There is no deception—only unconscious action. This shows us how easy it is for us to convince ourselves of something we want to be true.

- Perhaps we can't defend our free will very well, but at the very least we can learn a couple of habits to get better at thinking for ourselves. The first of these is learning to say no. This is tough for multiple reasons, but the solutions are plentiful. Start to say "I don't" versus "I can't," consider your beliefs about refusing people, resist the crucial moment of tension, and keep your thought process as nonpersonal as possible.

- The second habit to cultivate to think more rationally in the presence of others is to become an interrogator—that is, to ask questions about the source and the motives and to play devil's advocate to glean more information for yourself, and to stall while giving your rational mind time to overcome instinct.

- Inoculation theory is where you start to resist people's influences by exposing yourself to their arguments, specifically the weak parts, as much as possible beforehand. Once you can inoculate yourself against these persuasive angles and become adjusted to their impact and power, you can think more freely and avoid irrational decisions coming from people around you.

CHAPTER 3. THE EMOTIONS THAT RUN OUR LIVES

- Emotions are the cause of some of our weakest and most impulsive moments. This shouldn't be surprising—just consider how insane some of us act when mating and dating. That's because when emotions take over, they become our reality, and we just want to prolong positive emotions or immediately subdue painful ones.

- Paul Ekman defined six main emotions: happiness, sadness, anger, disgust, fear, and surprise. Too much of any of these can easily lead to irrational and harmful behaviors because emotions are all about instant, immediate, powerful actions. Those are not words typically associated with good decisions.

- Emotional arousal is connected with our instincts, which have remained with our species because in evolutionary terms, they helped us stay safe and survive. If we can understand these mechanisms behind, for example, love and fear, we can work *with* them rather than getting carried away with decisions that might not be in our best interests.

- To control our emotional arousal, we must increase the amount of the neurotransmitter GABA that is in our bloodstream. The easiest way to do this is through box breathing, which is simply taking twelve seconds for each complete breath.

- Human drives are perhaps the epitome of psychological triggers. They have kept our species alive, but those instincts don't transfer so well to the modern age. Thankfully, these human drives are relatively predictable because of how universal they are—within all people, and animals as well!
- The first human drive is selfishness and self-interest. We want to benefit from our behavior, and we want to benefit over other people. Not too surprising. Taken to the extreme, this drives us to antisocial and alienating behaviors.
- Another human drive is the preference for the path of least resistance. We seek the most benefit for the least amount of work on a consistent basis. Whether it's energy conservation or sloth, this is something that makes us act irrationally.

- ABCD—this is another model for human drives. It stands for acquire, bond, comprehend, and defend. Again, taken to the extreme, these can trigger all sorts of frightful behavior.
- Similarly, the classic seven sins represent things we want but shouldn't indulge in. You could probably classify them as psychological triggers themselves, which cause people to act irrationally.
- Maslow's famous theory shows us that human behavior is an attempt to satisfy various human needs, which fall on a hierarchy, with the most basic physiological and safety requirements needing to be fulfilled before we can consider the higher needs. The pinnacle is self-actualization, which is the point at which a human being fulfills their entire potential.
- The final natural human drive is self-defense—more specifically, defense of the ego and sense of pride. This is done through defense mechanisms, which actually skew your sense of reality. The

most widespread ones are denial, rationalization, and intellectualization.

- Our instincts have kept us alive thus far. Overall, it may be beneficial to have an "act first, think later" approach to life. But many of those actions and behaviors will inevitably be irrational or harmful because you are inherently acting with incomplete or imperfect information. So what do you do? Ignore what your gut tells you? Yes and no.
- Our gut feelings are formed largely by two psychological concepts: schemas and heuristics. Schemas are mental shortcuts that define our conception of a certain situation ("Based on what I see, what is happening here?") while heuristics are mental shortcuts that inform our place and role in certain situations ("Based on what I see, what should I be doing right now?"). They both work to eliminate decisions from your mental workload, but this isn't always beneficial. They are largely

269

subconscious and can lead to skewed realities if left uncorrected.

- Cognitive biases are additional ways our brain's propensity for shortcuts can harm us. They are errors in thinking that we struggle to see because our brains prefer to move ahead and ask questions later. Here, we only cover a few cognitive biases, though there are literally hundreds: preference for simplicity, reliance on contrast, and loss aversion.

- Finally, what can we do to battle these instincts that occasionally help us but harm us more often than not? Enter the six hats method of thinking, which encourages us to literally think about a situation or problem from six different perspectives. The creator, Edward de Bono, used colors, but avatars are a bit more helpful: Sherlock Holmes (gather information), Sigmund Freud (emotions), Eeyore the donkey (pessimist), a cheerleader (optimist), Pablo Picasso (creativity), and Henry Ford (information synthesis).

- The final set of psychological triggers that cause us to act irrationally are the human notions of free will and control over our destinies. What of it? Well, we like to feel that we have those things, even though we realistically don't. Our lives are more accurately deemed a set of random occurrences, opportunities, and chances. But that doesn't stop us from engaging in irrational behaviors that are detrimental, harmful, and self-defeating—all in the hope of gaining at most the illusion of control.

- Superstitions are the best example of wanting to gain the illusion of control. What won't we do for our favorite sports team to win? We go to great lengths with some of our rituals because we feel less tension with the world when it seems like we can affect outcomes or events.

- *Pareidolia* is the human tendency to see faces (i.e. patterns) where they don't exist. It's an extension of our natural desire to understand and make meaning

271

of the world, as well as to control, predict and master it. Our brains are always actively interpreting sense experiences and incoming data from the surrounding environment, often drawing conclusions and seeing connections or patterns that aren't actually there—something to be aware of if we wish to remain objective!

- Reactance theory is similar to reverse psychology. If you restrict someone's freedom or free will, they will feel triggered to demonstrate their agency to you. "Jane told me I can't do this, so I'm going to do it in front of her face." It's a powerful draw.

- So how do we deal with this lack of control in the universe? Are we to just accept that good things happen to bad people while bad things happen to good people, that there is no sense of cosmic justice and we are just a set of molecules and atoms that happen to be birthed into bodies? Yes and no. Acceptance is certainly part of the answer to keep you from acting irrationally in the pursuit of the illusion of control. But so is letting go, making sure not to give in to inaction, reflecting on past occurrences, and thinking through positive possibilities.

Printed in Great Britain
by Amazon